The

ELEVATED
COMMUNICATOR

The ELEVATED COMMUNICATOR

HOW TO MASTER YOUR STYLE and STRENGTHEN WELL-BEING AT WORK

MARYANNE O'BRIEN

SIMON ELEMENT

New York · London · Toronto · Sydney · New Delhi

SIMON
ELEMENT

An Imprint of Simon & Schuster, Inc.
1230 Avenue of the Americas
New York, NY 10020

First Simon Element trade paperback edition February 2023

SIMON ELEMENT is a trademark of Simon & Schuster, Inc.

For information about special discounts for bulk purchases, please contact Simon & Schuster Special Sales at 1-866-506-1949 or business@simonandschuster.com.

The Simon & Schuster Speakers Bureau can bring authors to your live event. For more information or to book an event, contact the Simon & Schuster Speakers Bureau at 1-866-248-3049 or visit our website at www.simonspeakers.com.

Manufactured in the United States of America

1   3   5   7   9   10   8   6   4   2

Library of Congress Control Number: 2021930550

ISBN 978-1-9821-5472-1
ISBN 978-1-9821-5473-8 (pbk)
ISBN 978-1-9821-5477-6 (ebook)

Contents

Contents

The
ELEVATED
COMMUNICATOR

Introduction

*W*e all want more meaning and purpose in our work. And understandably so! We give so much of ourselves to our jobs, and we need to know that what we do matters. We want to know that our work has a positive impact on another person, our team, our community, and the world around us. We feel it occasionally, but we want to experience meaning in some way, shape, or form every day.

In my life as a consultant, I spend a lot of time talking about "purpose." Why we need it, how we get it, where it comes from. Many people think that changing jobs or working for a nonprofit or purpose-driven company is the answer. They believe that if they can just find the *right* position, they'll feel fulfilled. But purpose doesn't live outside of us. Purpose lives *within* us and can be expressed every day through what we say and do. Ironically, we're searching for something that has always been within our reach.

In order to find purpose through our work, we have to be able to make genuine connections and build trusted relationships with other people. Our colleagues, our clients, the people we share office space with. Being authentic is the bedrock of our success and, yes, purpose. The problem is we're not always genuine at work. We fail to show up (or feel that we cannot show up) as our whole selves, and we fail to appreciate the connection between being ourselves, building trust, and feeling a sense of purpose. Like purpose, authenticity comes from a real place within us. We all know when someone is authentic and when they're not. We can feel it. Have you ever noticed that the people you enjoy working with the most are the ones you trust? When there's trust we feel safe enough to be ourselves. We're more open, creative, and productive, which enables us to have a positive impact on people through our work. And when there isn't trust, we end up avoiding people or in conflicts that cause our work and productivity to suffer.

Communication is essential for cultivating trust and finding meaning. It's central to everything we do. The modern workplace revolves around our ability to share ideas, provide direction, and collaborate. And most of us aren't very good communicators day in and day out. The vast majority of us operate with a gap between how we communicate when we're stressed and how we know we can communicate when our self-awareness and well-being are strong—and stress seems to be winning.

It comes as no surprise that we're burning out in record numbers. We're so stressed, anxious, and overwhelmed that it's impossible to perform at the level we're capable of. We go from meeting to meeting without taking a break. We don't even stop for lunch, let alone take a vacation day—there's always too much to do. We *need* to learn to take better care of ourselves! The path we're on is unsustainable. And it makes communication far more challenging, since we communicate at our level of well-being. This means that when we're healthy and energized (physically, emotionally, and mentally) we communicate far more effectively. And when we're not, we create more tension, conflict, and stress—and round and round we go. If you've ever found yourself feeling irritated, impatient, or quick to judge when you're tired and completely spent, then you know what I mean.

If we want to enjoy what we do (and we do!), we need to put our well-being on the front burner and make it a priority. We need to invest in ourselves and raise our baseline level of well-being so we can communicate and collaborate more effectively and find more meaning in our work.

BECOMING AN ELEVATED COMMUNICATOR

You'd think that given the importance of communication skills—and the fact that being successful in nearly every job revolves around our ability to get along well with people and build trust—that we'd make communication a higher priority. But the truth is that many of our priorities have been upside down for far too long. We've been taught by our parents, managers, and society to believe that playing the game, with all of its managing up, 24/7 availability, and office politics, is how you "win." But if you've been in the workplace for any length of time, you already know that this approach is completely backward.

When we focus on managing up or making ourselves look good, we come across as disingenuous to our coworkers. When we fail to unplug and restore we drain our reserves, becoming more prone to stress, miscommunication, and conflict. And when we play the political game, we stop being ourselves, we don't say what we really think, and we succumb to power plays that damage our relationships. There isn't one successful or satisfying quality in the bunch. This behavior only serves to produce more tension, erode trust, and make it that much more difficult to find meaning in our work.

Imagine how much more effective we'd be if we turned the tables to upend the current model. What if we instilled the belief that it's everyone's responsibility to take care of their well-being? What if we were all genuine with each other? What if we valued managing down more than managing up? What if we all modeled accountability and treated everyone with respect? What if we used our ability to positively impact people and feel more purpose every day? Things would certainly be much better.

We'd set boundaries and take time to recharge, so we could show up positive, energized, and with an open mind. We'd create the bandwidth we need to be patient and listen. And we'd be much more willing to share information, collaborate, and problem-solve.

This is just a glimpse into the environment we can create when we get our priorities straight, communicate effectively, and build trust. And from this glimpse it's easy to see that when we create this kind of working environment, we're set up to experience true success: we'd enjoy going to work and find meaning through the positive impact we create all around us.

Sometimes we forget that cultures are made up of people (like us) and that how we show up makes a significant difference. The truth is that *the change we want to experience begins with us*. And since we all have the ability to change, it's simply a matter of tapping into the power and potential that lives within us.

Over the years I've worked with dozens of purpose-driven organizations—filled with well-intentioned people who wanted to make a difference—and it wasn't their desire or ability that got in their way. Inevitably, it was communication. Yes, it's our inability to genuinely connect with people, to build trust, to collaborate, and to take responsibility for our behavior that ultimately prevents us from thriving, accessing our potential, and experiencing well-being at work.

Elevated communicators possess a high level of self-awareness and personal responsibility. They have the courage and confidence to be genuine and open-minded. They can talk about any issue without becoming defensive or judgmental. They recognize what people need to be at their best and flex their style to put them at ease. And, most important, they look for every opportunity to create a positive impact and find meaning through their work. Becoming an elevated communicator doesn't happen overnight. It's a journey of personal growth and transformation—one that allows you to see who you are today and who you're capable of being.

Like improving any skill, elevating your communication is a process. You learn to truly understand who you are and how you impact people. You learn to express yourself in a way that brings out the best in you and others. You learn to continually invest in raising your baseline level of self-awareness and well-being. You learn to consciously choose your response and take responsibility for what you say and do. And you learn to intentionally build trusted working relationships with all kinds of people.

WHY I WROTE THIS BOOK

I've spent my entire career in the field of communication, and I've seen how powerful it can be. It has the ability to bring us together and make us more effective. It can also divide us and make work more complicated. The difference comes down to us—how well we understand ourselves, what drives the way we communicate, and how we impact others. And how we use that understanding to evolve and grow.

If you want to bring out the best in yourself and create a positive impact through your work, communication is the most important skill you can develop. It's foundational to every other soft skill—like teamwork, creative thinking, problem solving, or conflict resolution—and central to every job. It might sound strange to think that developing skills such as listening, positivity, and curiosity can have such a profound impact on our sense of purpose and well-being at work, but it's true. In my consulting and coaching work, I've helped leaders, teams, boards, and organizations to strengthen their communication skills and I've seen people and companies completely transform—we're talking a 180-degree shift. I've seen leaders raise their self-awareness and change their ways. I've seen trust rebuilt where it had been lost. And I've seen people who used to complain about their jobs find true satisfaction in them—all through the power of elevating their communication skills.

There's nothing more inspiring than to see someone continuously evolving into better versions of themselves. We all have so much unrealized potential. We just need a little support to be able to really see ourselves and recognize that we have the ability to change whatever it is that isn't working. You can shift the quality of your relationships and how you experience work every day—and that's my hope for you. But most of all, I hope that this book can help you understand yourself better. Self-awareness is the foundation of all positive change; the more you learn, and the more you commit to the process of self-discovery, the more you set yourself up for success.

In an effort to help people see their habits and tendencies more clearly, I've used style assessments with my clients. On the one hand, these were often very effective: They held up an objective perspective, gave organizations a common language, and helped deepen self-understanding without self-judgment. At the same time, I found myself continually frustrated that there wasn't an effective assessment geared specifically toward how we communicate at work. I was working with a client to build their organization's communication skills when I began to see the need for something different from what already existed. And so I set out to create an assessment that would help people really understand their communication style and how it impacts their ability to connect with people. I wanted a tool that specifically focused on how we communicate at work, since how we express ourselves outside of work is often quite different; one that went deep into the complexities of the beliefs, values, behaviors, and attitudes that shape the way we communicate.

DISCOVERING COMMUNICATION STYLES

In the quantitative research my team and I conducted, we discovered four unique communication styles: expressive, reserved, direct, and harmonious. Each style is a constellation of distinct clusters of habitual behaviors across three dimensions: assertiveness, collaboration, and consideration.

You'll get to know your style through the profiles that bring your defining characteristics, behaviors, patterns, and attitudes to life. You'll see that each style has a range of expressions that's shaped by our level of self-awareness and well-being, which tend to fluctuate. They provide insights into what motivates you, how you engage, and how you impact others.

Have you ever found that you sometimes shift the way you communicate at work, depending on the situation or who you're talking to? So did we! There are simply too many layers to who we are and how we interact to be defined by a single style. This is why the algorithm in the Communication Style Assessment gives you both your primary and secondary style. The combination of your styles helps you to really understand your strengths and weaknesses, your skills and vulnerabilities. You begin to fully see where you shine and where you may be getting in your own way.

LET'S GET STARTED

Remember, communication is a skill. This means that everyone has the ability to become an elevated communicator. If you truly want to improve your communication skills, you need to understand what influences the way you communicate today. So, as tempting as it might be to jump straight into understanding your style, don't. Take your time. Read through Part 1. It's filled with information you need to know in order to better understand yourself, and if you skip it, this is most likely where you're going to get tripped up.

It teaches you how to rewire your brain so that the practices and techniques you learn—and put into action—become habits that make communicating at a higher level feel effortless. You'll see that, at first, you need to take what you learn and intentionally put the ideas into practice—it's what you do. Then, over time, your practice will become second nature and you won't have to think about it—it will simply be who you are now. This is how you create sustainable change and continue to access more of your potential.

Before you dive in, go to TheElevatedCommunicator.com and take the assessment to discover your primary and secondary communication styles so you can keep them in mind while reading Part 1.

And just in case I haven't emphasized it enough, please start at the beginning of the book and apply the ideas as you go. When you learn the practices and techniques for becoming a better listener, use them. When you learn about why we all get triggered, start looking for what sets you off and why. When you learn about the strengths of your style, start leaning on them more often. All of the small changes that you make along the way add up. And before you know it, you'll be operating on a whole new level of communication and finding more meaning in your work every day!

Part 1

Communication Influences

CHAPTER 1

Communication Is at the
Heart of Our Success

*W*hen you think about it, nearly all of our work revolves around communication in some form. It doesn't matter what line of work you're in, it's hard to imagine a day where we don't connect with someone through emails, texts, or phone calls. We routinely run meetings, give and receive feedback, and facilitate brainstorms. In fact, we communicate so frequently that we rarely give it much consideration. But we should. How we communicate influences everything, from how effectively we build relationships to our level of personal well-being.

Communication is so central to every job that it continually tops the list of what recruiters and employers from around the world look for when hiring.[1] Every company wants to hire people who can present their ideas clearly, listen effectively, and work collaboratively. So, it only makes sense that the more effectively we communicate the more success we experience. All the intelligence in the world won't help you if you can't get your point across and connect with people.

If you've ever felt uneasy sharing your ideas, expressing a differing point of view, or addressing conflict you know that communication isn't always natural

11

and easy. The truth is that soft skills are hard. They require the ability to really understand yourself and others. Anyone who has ever worked to develop their emotional intelligence (EQ) or leadership skills knows that the human side of work is complicated and necessitates the ability to communicate well. This is why communication reigns supreme when it comes to soft skills; it's at the foundation of them all. When you have strong communication skills you can read other people's behavior, avoid and resolve conflict, discuss issues and make decisions, and listen well. The paradox is that while communication is clearly one of the most important skills you can develop, few people invest much time or effort honing this skill.

Remember, the ability to communicate effectively isn't a personality trait that you either have or you don't. It's a learned skill that we can all develop and master through conscious effort and experience. Increasingly, organizations depend on information sharing and collaboration to achieve their goals. This is why communication is considered an essential life skill—it's critical for building strong interpersonal skills and trusted working relationships.

GENUINE COMMUNICATION
BUILDS TRUST

Trust is one of the essential elements that holds our relationships together. When trust is present we feel safe, which allows us to genuinely connect and work well together. When we're sincere, respectful, and transparent we inspire trust. When we lie, manipulate, or withhold information we damage trust. Pretty straightforward, right? Even so, in many cultures these destructive behaviors happen all too often. Some people fail to realize that without trust there's no relationship. And at the risk of stating the obvious, having trusted working relationships is critical to how work gets done.

As a consultant, I'm often brought in to work with organizations where trust is low and the toxic fallout is beginning to affect the whole organization. Invariably, there's a communication issue that needs to be resolved. I've worked with leaders who were more comfortable controlling than trusting. Teams where one or two dominant voices drown out all the others. Colleagues who were quick to judge and slow to open up to new perspectives. I've seen people become manipulative when they feel threatened and others who shut down, doing the bare minimum to keep from being fired.

I've also seen the worst possible situations turn around—a complete 180-degree shift—when people learn to genuinely communicate and work to rebuild trust. Granted, it takes some willingness and flexibility, but people are often motivated by the fact that they want to get promoted or stay employed. Plus, most people aren't looking for more conflict. Most of the time they just haven't been able to see or acknowledge how they're contributing to the problem—we all have blind spots and blaming others is easier than seeing ourselves fully. Some people have no idea how they're coming across, especially when they're under stress; in these situations, raising their self-awareness and well-being makes all the difference. Other times, there's a disparity in how individuals are communicating (what I call a "style gap") that needs to be bridged to avoid creating additional tension and misunderstandings.

Every communication style has a range of expressions that spans from healthy (on our best days) to stressed (on our worst days). Where we fall on that spectrum has a lot to do with how well we take care of ourselves. When we make it a point to get a good night's sleep, create a positive mindset, and play to our strengths we move into the healthy zone: we listen, stay open, and thoughtfully respond. And when we're exhausted and overwhelmed, we slip into stress mode: we become blunt, impatient, judgmental, and reactive.

The goal is to gradually move your autopilot mode (how you act day in and day out) toward the healthiest expression of your style and narrow the gap between your actions when you're healthy and stressed. That way you're at your best more often than not. Just to be clear, operating from your healthiest, most Zen self 100% of the time is not the goal. That would be an outrageous expectation! Can you imagine never feeling irritated or making a sarcastic remark ever again in your life? But with some simple interventions and a little dedication you can learn to recognize when you're in danger of widening that communication gap and take the necessary steps to care for yourself so that you can communicate from a healthier place, have a positive impact on the people around you, and build trust.

There are few forces as powerful as trust when it comes to cementing relationships. It's also a choice: We choose to be sincere, respectful, and transparent. We choose to be genuine—to be open, respond honestly, and listen with curiosity. As you begin to understand your communication style (which we'll explore in more detail in Part 2), you'll become increasingly aware of how you communicate and connect with others at your best. And you'll gain insight into how you can authentically build trust with people whose communication needs differ from yours. By simply taking someone's style needs into consideration you can help put them at ease and create smoother interactions.

WELL-BEING AFFECTS OUR LEVEL OF COMMUNICATION

Communication challenges abound when we're feeling overwhelmed and/or failing to care for our physical and emotional needs. When our stress goes up our ability to communicate goes down. We become more emotional and reactive, and everyone has their own way of handling it. Some of us bulldoze over people to get our way or become argumentative and go on the attack to squash any dissension. And others may withdraw and/or become highly emotional.

> I'm very conflict-averse. When tension starts to build, I shut down pretty quickly and go silent. My flight impulse is really strong and all I want to do is leave. And if I'm at a point where the stress is overflowing and I can't leave, out come the tears.
>
> —Emily (Harmonious)

We all become more sensitive when we're exhausted and pushing through. Stress activates our reptilian brains, which puts us into fight, flight, or freeze. This makes it difficult to process what we're feeling or see what's really driving us. Our self-awareness seems to go right out the window and we become triggered more quickly. We're quick to judge ourselves and others, taking things personally and projecting rampantly. It's only through reflection that we can see things more clearly.

When I'm feeling a lot of stress or direct conflict, I can get defensive and find myself playing the victim or blaming others. Recently, I was leading a project and feeling anxious about it. I was struggling to advance, and it brought up a lot of self-doubt. When a colleague shared critical feedback, I immediately interpreted it as an attack. Instead of being open to the conversation, I withdrew—both in my body language and my lack of response. I felt myself taking the feedback personally and allowed it to exacerbate my existing self-doubt, which wasn't productive or helpful—for me, the team, or the project.

—Ayme (Expressive)

Poor communication keeps us stuck in an endless energy-draining cycle that leaves us emotionally depleted. But when we learn to recognize our communication patterns under stress, we can address the stress dynamics before they play out and choose a new response. As our self-awareness rises, we begin to better understand ourselves and what's driving us. We're able to see how we're expressing ourselves and impacting others. We can see the influences and dynamics between people and identify how to handle the situation. And, perhaps most important, we show empathy and compassion for others.

When I'm calm and tuned in, I love to support my team. For example, I have one team member who gets nervous whenever he's presenting . . . his delivery shifts into this flat mode and it makes everyone uncomfortable. When this starts to happen, I find a natural opening to interject with a supportive comment to connect the dots in a new way that adds a little life to what he's saying. This immediately puts him at ease and makes things conversational again. My ability to see what people need and address it in the moment builds my team's trust and confidence in me. When my team performs well and we're able to help our clients, I feel successful and that motivates me.

—Tara (Expressive)

When we're feeling calm and centered, it's much easier to see and sync up with people's needs. Without stress nagging at our self-preservation instincts, we can focus on others and align our actions with the subtle cues they're sending. For example, have you ever found yourself adjusting your pace—picking it up or slowing it down—depending on who you're talking to? Or maybe you see your team's furtive glances during a meeting and pause an extra moment to allow quieter voices to join the conversation? These simple but significant changes in how we communicate build relationships that foster trust and a sense of belonging.

WE'RE BETTER TOGETHER

It's hardly surprising that some of our strongest professional relationships become friendships that extend outside of work seeing as we spend more time at work than anywhere else. We come to care about our friends at work and want to know about their lives. And it's often the people we work with that keep us showing up day after day.

Some people love to build personal relationships with everyone, and others prefer to build just a few friendships and to keep things more professional. No matter where you fall on this spectrum, the science is clear that there are enormous benefits to developing positive social relationships at work. According to Gallup's 30+ year study, those of us who have a best friend at work are seven times as likely to be engaged in our jobs, produce higher-quality work, and have a greater sense of well-being.[2]

Then there's the fact that psychologists have long recognized that we have a strong, innate desire to feel connected to people. You've likely heard that your relationships will make or break your career. But more important, the quality of your relationships can make or break your life.

We're born with a desire to connect with people. Our relationships fulfill our need to feel safe and belong, and they strengthen our well-being. In fact, the field of positive psychology has repeatedly shown that developing interpersonal skills and building positive relationships significantly impacts our physical and mental health. When we have positive social experiences—celebrating a coworker's birthday, a team lunch, or an inspiring ideation—the brain releases oxytocin, a powerful hormone that's linked to trustworthiness and motivation to help others at work.[3] The more relationships we build that are cooperative, fair, and trusted, the more often we activate this reward pathway in the brain. This cycle promotes continued trust, respect, and confidence between us. It also shifts our mindset from competitive to collaborative, where we believe in and inspire each other to be at our best.[4]

We all know that we're more likely to share an idea or voice an opinion in a meeting with people we like and trust. We know we'll be supported and enjoy the discussions that make our ideas better. These experiences boost both our confidence and our well-being. In fact, every positive interaction we have at work directly affects the body's physiological processes, fortifying our cardio-vascular, immune, and neuroendocrine systems against the damaging effects of stress. Simply put, positive working relationships enhance our body's ability to build, maintain, and repair itself—both at work and at home.[5]

We're at our best—physically, emotionally, and mentally—when we come together and support one another. So even if it's not your thing to build a life-time supply of deep friendships at work, there are plenty of reasons to stay open to the idea and experiment with it a bit. You might even find that you're pleas-antly surprised by the results.

MIND THE GAP

Given all the remarkable things that good communication can do for us, and how important we all acknowledge it to be, you'd think more of us would be better communicators. But the reality is most of us operate with a pretty big gap between how we're capable of communicating and the everyday reality of how we interact with people. We interrupt when we should be listening. We're critical instead of being open-minded. We feign agreement rather than raising an important issue.

Sometimes we don't fully realize that we're doing it until after the fact. Have you ever looked back on a conversation and wondered, *What happened there? Why did I say that?* We go in with the intention to patiently listen and support our team but end up cutting people off, using "tone," or saying nothing in order to keep things moving.

These gaps are caused by a combination of high stress, low well-being, and low self-awareness. In the moment, the pressure gets to us and we emotionally react. We can't see that we're making matters worse. And if we can't see it, we can't stop it.

ELEVATING COMMUNICATION SKILLS AND CLOSING THE GAP

The good news is we're not just leaves blowing helplessly in the wind unable to choose how we respond to our environment. We have the ability to change how we communicate. Day by day, conversation by conversation, you can make small changes that will lead to big shifts in the way you connect with people.

Ultimately, becoming an elevated communicator is about closing the communication gap and building trusted relationships that make work more enjoyable and satisfying. It's about learning to intentionally engage with others with a high level of self-awareness, empathy, and flexibility—even when stress is high. We're human, so we'll never be perfect, but we can continue to improve, grow, and evolve.

The first step is to understand the role the brain plays in shaping the way we communicate. When you learn to recognize your unconscious patterns, triggers, and the signals your central nervous system sends, you can use this information to change your response and dissolve patterns that limit the way you think, feel, and express yourself. You can intentionally engage with people and become a more effective communicator—listen to differing perspectives without becoming defensive, say what you think without pushing, and be authentic in every conversation. No matter what line of work you're in, communication is critical to your success. When you invest in elevating your communication skills, you raise your value and expand your impact.

CHAPTER 2

Meet Your Brain

*M*any of us live with the illusion that we control how we communicate with people, but the reality is that the vast majority of the time we're simply following how our brains have been programmed to respond. Over the past several decades, a number of scientific breakthroughs have radically changed our understanding about how the brain works. These discoveries have helped us to better understand how the conscious and subconscious minds work to protect each other from the overload of information that flows in each day; how our DNA comes imprinted with ancestral patterning that directs our behaviors; why we get emotionally triggered; and how to rewire our brain through conscious awareness to disrupt the habitual behaviors that keep us from experiencing life the way we want to.

The good news is that we have the ability to rewire our minds, change our behaviors, and shift how we interact with people. This means that as we become aware of where we need to improve, we can make some simple adjustments (and bigger changes) to close the gaps that keep us from communicating effectively and genuinely connecting with others.

We all have communication filters, patterns, and habits that influence the way our brains process information. And while it's true that we all have the same basic hardware (a brain), our brains are all wired uniquely such that we all see the world through our own software lens. The operating system behind it is grounded in beliefs. Whether you're aware of it or not, you operate at the level of your beliefs. Some make us more effective and others hold us back, filling our minds with thoughts that limit our potential and keep us stuck—for example, beliefs like "It's best to lay low when conflict arises" or "If I say what I really think, people won't like me." This line of thinking prevents us from taking risks, growing, and expanding our comfort zone. We have a whole range of unconscious programs that create our reality, telling us what to pay attention to or how to respond—and we follow their lead. In fact, most of the time our subconscious programs are running the show and directing how we communicate when we're on autopilot. It's one of the ways we manage the expectation to "always be on" and deal with the unending streams of information flowing in. Autopilot is a protective mechanism that limits how much information we consciously process. In familiar situations, our instinctual ways of interacting take over and we fall into a rhythm that requires very little thinking at all. When our subconscious programming has been intentionally designed to bring out the best in us and others, we're set up for success. And when it's not, we have a bit of work to do to communicate effectively.

The more you understand what shapes the way you communicate, the more you can optimize your strengths and intentionally program your thoughts and responses to create positive and authentic connections with people. It's reassuring to know that you can consciously change the way you express yourself. The first step is always to better understand yourself: how you're wired, what triggers you, and how you can change what isn't working for you.

HERE'S HOW WE'RE WIRED

Have you ever been in a meeting and found your mind wandering while people are talking? Of course you have; we all do it! Before we even realize it, we've slipped into an automatic response mode, where we barely pay attention to the conversation until a point is directed toward us. The reality is that most of our everyday interactions happen on autopilot—when we engage or respond without giving too much thought to what we're saying or how we're coming across.

The reason is that our conscious mind—the part that's creative, discerning, and rational—has a surprisingly low threshold in terms of what it can be aware of before it becomes overwhelmed.

The subconscious mind, on the other hand, is like a giant supercomputer that has an unlimited capacity for storage and exceptional processing speed. The conscious mind delegates as much as it can to the subconscious mind so that it's free to deal with the big stuff. In fact, it's quite good at delegating. Neuroscientists estimate that the conscious mind is only directing and controlling our response about 5% of the time, leaving the subconscious mind running the show the other 95%.[1]

By and large, this is a good thing. Our subconscious stops our conscious brains from overloading: Can you imagine how taxing it would be if you had to consciously think about every simple daily action—like how to brush your teeth, make coffee, or use the remote every time you wanted to watch TV? Ideally, your subconscious programming is in harmony with your conscious mind—meaning that your automatic reactions are aligned with what you'd say and do if you were intentionally responding. This is absolutely possible, especially in communication, though most of us still have some work to do to identify and repair the faulty programming.

Let's expand on the computer metaphor to anchor a few more important functions of the brain. The conscious mind is a creative mind—it has the ability to choose and create responses from our intentions, aspirations, and desires. And the subconscious mind is a programmed mind—it doesn't think or reason independently, it obeys the commands of the conscious mind and operates from habit. This means that the conscious mind acts as the software that programs the supercomputer that is your subconscious mind. Your subconscious is where all your experiences are stored; its main function is to record and play back information. What's fascinating is that it's unable to discern the truth from a lie; it simply believes everything you tell it. And it doesn't think in words, it sees in pictures.

Over the course of your life your subconscious mind has been permanently filing away every memory with an image. Each of those memories is connected to people, places, and situations from your past and filled with emotions, which are the ultimate end product of your past experiences. So, the moment your brain recalls a memory it's retrieved like a mini movie, wrapped in images and packed with emotion. This is why under hypnosis people can often remember, with perfect clarity, events from decades before. It's also why your memories have the power to transport you into the joy or pain of that experience.

Conscious Mind	Subconscious Mind
5%	95%
Awareness	Autopilot
Creativity and imagination	Programs and habits
Discerning	Unquestioning
Reason and logic	Emotions and stories

Ultimately, our subconscious programming directs how we think, feel, behave, and communicate. And while much of our wiring was in place long before we developed the capability of conscious thought, we have the ability to find and fix bugs in the system.

EARLY COMMUNICATION PROGRAMMING

Upon arrival, our brain is already encoded with operating instructions—prewired circuitry that holds the memories and experiences of our parents, grandparents, great-grandparents, and beyond. Scientists believe that the ancestral programming in our DNA goes back fourteen generations or more.[2]

Have you ever had a friend of your family tell you how much you remind them of one of your parents? When I was growing up, I was often told "Your ability to persuade [read: get your way] reminds me of your father; he could talk anyone into anything." My father died when I was just two, and I never understood how I could be like someone I didn't remember. It wasn't until I learned about inherited communication qualities that it made sense. How we communicate is a combination of our genetic neural circuitry, the encoded memories from our own experiences, and the beliefs that shape how we operate. Maybe you've already noticed how you unconsciously say things that remind you of what your mother or father said to you growing up. It's practically a rite of passage to find yourself saying "I've turned into my mother/father." Now you know why.

The next phase of subconscious programming happens during the first seven years of life. Up until age seven our brain operates at a theta frequency that's associated with the state of hypnosis; it lives just below conscious awareness. As a child the brain is designed to download the programs needed to survive by observing and absorbing the behaviors of our parents, siblings, friends, coaches, teachers, and community. Whether it was spoken aloud or relayed in subtle cues, they told us what was right and wrong, when to speak up and when to be quiet, what was acceptable and what was not. Whatever people said or did, the subconscious recorded it as truth, and this became the programming for your beliefs and behaviors—because, again, the subconscious believes *everything* it's told. The problem is that much of the programming we absorb is flawed. In fact, studies show that 70% of the programs we download from others are negative, disempowering, and self-sabotaging.[3] What makes this extremely relevant is that these faulty programs drive 95% of our behavior.

Michelle was a precocious and curious young girl. She bombarded her parents with questions on a daily basis. She vividly remembers being told, "Would you stop asking so many questions? It's exhausting!" And she finally did. It had become clear that people didn't like it when she asked questions, and she took it to mean that it must somehow be bad.

As an adult this became an issue for her at work. She would hesitate to ask questions when she didn't understand a project, which led to mistakes and delays. She was uncomfortable asking questions in meetings and her colleagues became frustrated with her lack of engagement. Thankfully, with some coaching, she was able to see that she had imprinted a faulty program and a limiting belief; asking questions isn't inherently bad.

We all have memories and stories that shape the way we see the world. They can be quite helpful when they reinforce our positive characteristics and supportive beliefs. Replaying experiences in which you overcame adversity boosts your resilience. Recalling the sense of belonging you felt as a member of your hockey team strengthens your belief in the power of teamwork. And memories that connect you to times when you felt recognized and appreciated build your confidence and sense of self-worth.

At the other end of the spectrum are the negative experiences that affect our view of the world. People who suffered verbal abuse from their parents, coaches, or authority figures are often afraid to speak up at work. People who participated in team projects in high school or college where others didn't pull their weight tend to be distrustful when working collaboratively as adults. And anyone who has endured an embarrassment while presenting in front of a group knows how challenging it can be to stand up and speak in public, even decades later.

As we become consciously aware of the stories that inform our communication patterns, we're able to see with greater clarity how the early influences of our family, friends, culture, and emotional memories inform how we communicate— our mannerisms, our level of empathy, how personable we are, the strength of our opinions, and how much anxiety we feel when speaking up. Given that we all have some faulty programming, it's important to check in periodically to see if we're accurately perceiving our world. This is especially important when we feel tired, stressed, and overwhelmed, because this is when we're more likely to see things through a distorted lens.

WE SEE WHAT WE EXPECT TO SEE

Scientists used to believe that the way we responded to situations was based on the information flowing into the brain from the outside world. They thought that our brains simply took in information, processed it, assigned meaning, and directed our thinking and behavior as a result. But it turns out they had it all backward.

Here's how things really work: the brain looks for what it has been conditioned to expect, based on a combination of our personal and inherited beliefs and experiences. Within the brain is a filtering system called the reticular activating system (RAS) that protects us from information overload. The RAS is a bundle of nerves located at your brain stem that filters out massive amounts of sensory information. Scientists estimate that the unconscious mind has the ability to process roughly 11 million bits of information *per second*, but the conscious mind can only process roughly 50 to 100 bits per second. As the gatekeeper of information, the RAS decides what's allowed into your conscious mind, based on your beliefs, perceptions, and priorities.[4] By filtering out unnecessary information, your conscious attention can then be drawn to what's really important. This is how we know to ignore a car horn in the distance but look up when the car is barreling down our path.

The subconscious mind is always reading the world around us, trying to interpret how to navigate every situation based on a long list of preexisting beliefs, stories, stereotypes, and biases. And as the subconscious runs its predictive program, it directs our attention to what we expect to see and experience. It selectively sorts the information and allows in only what reinforces what we already think. Once our view is confirmed, the brain actually stops gathering data, simply ignoring new information that disproves our beliefs. It's called *confirmation bias* and is largely responsible for why we see what we look for.[5]

Sporting events provide ample evidence of confirmation bias. A study of Dartmouth and Princeton football fans, who were asked to watch the same tape of a particularly bitter rivalry game, found that a person's opinion fundamentally directed how they viewed the game. They found:

> Despite the constancy of the objective stimulus, the opposing partisans' assessments of what they had viewed suggested that they "saw" two different games. The Princeton fans saw a continuing saga of Dartmouth atrocities and occasional Princeton retaliations. The Dartmouth fans saw brutal Princeton provocations and occasional measured Dartmouth responses. Each side, in short, saw a struggle in which their side were the "good guys" and the other side were the "bad guys." And each side thought this "truth" ought to be apparent to any objective observers of the same events.[6]

In short, the fans were predisposed to see their team in a positive light, so their interpretation of the game supported that belief.

The upside of confirmation bias, of course, is that it wires us for efficiency. It would be exhausting to critically evaluate every bit of information to make an unbiased decision or navigate every situation, so we operate using pattern recognition and anticipation programming. We do it at work all the time, especially when it comes to how we interact with people. Have you ever walked into a room and instantly recognized that someone's upset before they've said a word? Or maybe you've noticed that when you're sharing a new idea you already know who will be supportive and who will push back. We unconsciously categorize people and their behaviors and use that information to direct how we engage with them.

The problem is that, like our subconscious, confirmation bias is far from foolproof. While it does allow us to move through our days without being completely overwhelmed by trying to anticipate every encounter, we're far from perfect when it comes to our perceptions. It takes conscious effort to discern truth from bias, especially since we tend to trust that the things we see and directly experience are accurate. Rarely do we stop to question how we're perceiving things, even though we should. Instead, we simply assume our stories and conclusions are spot-on.

We're predisposed to see and hear what confirms our feelings about a situation or relationship. Think about how differently you behave in conversations with people you trust than with those you don't. When there is trust, we believe that people are sincere and reliable, and so that's what we see. When they ask clarifying questions, it's engagement. And when they want to discuss project timing, they're simply being responsible. Now run that same conversation through your filter for someone you don't trust, and questions are likely to be perceived as challenges, and any talk of moving the timeline is an indication of laziness. Whether we're aware of it or not, we see what we believe and expect to see.

When you understand how your subconscious programming influences the way you interpret information, make decisions, and communicate, it's easy to see the importance of learning to question your stories, assumptions, and beliefs.

This is why it's so important to look within, strengthen your self-awareness, and learn to recognize when your view of people and situations has become too narrow. It's also a good way to test what kind of an echo chamber you've created for yourself, because we all do it.

Practice listening to the stories you tell yourself. Take a closer look at what you say about yourself and others and see if you can identify the beliefs and assumptions that create the narratives that run through your mind. If you have a journal or a mindfulness practice, spend some time reflecting on the stories that come up most often for you in stressful work situations. Look at when they tend to appear and see if you can trace your story back to where it all began.

When the subconscious mind employs confirmation bias, it significantly influences how we communicate, build relationships, and feel about ourselves. It also has the power to solidify how you see yourself in ways that can lift you up or pull you down. Let's take public speaking as an example. Objectively, presenting is a skill that anyone can develop. But when your beliefs and emotions drive your thinking, you see presenting through the lens of how you've performed in the past. Say you believe that you're a great presenter and have received lots of positive feedback throughout your career. When it comes time to pitch a new marketing campaign, you're likely to present with more authority, charm, and grace. You develop the ability to land your points with finesse, finding just the right words, inflection, and pacing to emotionally connect with your clients. While you're presenting, your brain filters in more proof points—people smiling, nodding, and laughing—which tell you you're doing a great job. This boosts your confidence and makes you enjoy speaking even more. Conversely, if you believe you're a terrible presenter, you're more likely to forget every point you wanted to land and perceive a questioning expression as doubt rather than curiosity. You might stumble throughout your delivery and project insecurity. And when you're finally finished, you obsess over everything that went wrong, replaying every mistake and reinforcing your belief in your poor speaking skills.

Since our self-perceptions keep us stuck in patterns of thinking and cycles of behavior, it's essential that we're able see the best in ourselves and pay attention to when we're being overly critical. These same dynamics hold true for how we perceive others. As soon as we judge or categorize someone (which we do all the time), that's all we see. Have you ever met someone who immediately made you feel uneasy? They were too candid, too agreeable, too open—and that experience imprinted your perception of them. This is why making a first impression is so important and why it can be so hard to correct a bad one. However, when we become consciously aware of the beliefs and biases that shape the way we view people and situations, we can see how faulty programming can have a cumulative effect that negatively impacts our working relationships, performance, and well-being.[7]

WE ALL GET TRIGGERED

You know that feeling when someone says something that hits a nerve and immediately destabilizes you? One minute you're feeling fine and the next you're suddenly spiraling in a tornado of anger, panic, guilt, or shame? That's an emotional trigger. We all have them and for the most part our triggers stem from our childhood, when we invariably had emotionally impactful experiences that we either couldn't acknowledge or deal with at the time. The more a trigger was repeated, the more it was reinforced in our subconscious mind and the more vigilant your nervous system becomes when you're in similar—and thereby potentially threatening—situations.

For example, my friend James was raised in a home filled with tension. His father was an alcoholic and his parents fought constantly, so he grew up fearing and avoiding conflict. Today, he still gets painfully triggered at the hint of tension at work. His body sounds an alarm: anxiety bubbles up in the pit of his stomach and it becomes difficult to breathe or think clearly. Whenever a conversation becomes too intense, or colleagues get into a heated debate, those same feelings of fear and discomfort he had as a child are activated.

We all have emotional responses that hijack our brain when we're triggered. This is because the brain is emotionally wired for fear, so our immediate reaction to any event is always going to be emotional. There's no way around this. It's an instinctual and ancient response intended to protect us in life-and-death situations. Our self-preservation instinct keeps us intensely attuned to potential threats; if you're triggered, you *will* have a physical and emotional response. Even so, that doesn't mean we're at the mercy of our triggers. Over time, and through new experiences, we can teach ourselves that our fear response is misplaced: the threat we perceive isn't actually a real threat to our safety.

Every message you receive from your senses and environment enters through the thalamus, which acts as the brain's relay station. The thalamus forwards the message to one of two places. One is the amygdala, your emotional brain and fear center. The other is the prefrontal cortex, which is home to your intellect and spirit.

When the thalamus senses danger, it relays sensory information simultaneously to both the neocortex and the amygdala. It arrives at the amygdala first, since it has a direct path; there's a tiny neural thread (wire) that runs directly between your thalamus and your amygdala. Almost immediately, the amygdala floods your system with adrenaline and cortisol to prepare your body for fight, flight, or freeze. This causes a cascade of hormones that produce well-orchestrated physiological changes. Your heart begins to pound and your muscles tense. Your breathing quickens and beads of sweat appear. As your body prepares to protect itself, emotional thoughts race in, fueling anxiety (anger, shame, guilt, etc.), which takes on a life of its own and clouds your thinking.

Meanwhile, that urgent "DANGER, DANGER!" message has made its way to your prefrontal cortex, where the full power of evaluation and reason are underway, exploring better options than fighting, running away, or freezing on the spot. It consults the amygdala while rationally evaluating the best approach. Thankfully, scientists have found that there's a critical lag time between the urge to take action and when you actually follow through: a full quarter-second delay that creates a window during which your prefrontal cortex empowers you to disengage from the physiological reactions in your body and choose your response.[8] This means that we're not at the mercy of the emotional response that's underway; *we have the power to choose our response when we're triggered.* And while a quarter of a second may not sound like a lot of time, it's practically infinite when you realize the massive computing power of your brain.

It's plenty of time to question whether you're perceiving a situation accurately. It's plenty of time to realize that the comment was a joke and not meant to hurt your feelings, or that the question was designed to spark conversation and not judgmental, or that stumbling over a slide can be funny rather than humiliating. It's plenty of time to hear your story and ask yourself if it's true or not. And when you learn to recognize your triggers, you can take advantage of this split-second window to choose your response.

If we decide to remain on autopilot and allow ourselves to be swept away by our emotional reactions, things tend to go from bad to worse. When the amygdala is constantly allowed to hijack the brain it becomes overly sensitive, which makes it more and more capable of taking control. Every time a neural pathway is used it becomes easier and faster to travel; it's like expanding a dirt road into a six-lane freeway through repetitive use. Pretty soon, you're flying down an emotional highway unencumbered by rational thought.

People who never work to manage their emotional triggers lose their ability to accurately perceive things. Have you ever worked with someone where you feel like you're always walking on eggshells, where you're careful to avoid setting them off? They're highly reactive and overly emotional. They take things more personally. They snap without notice. When people operate on this level it's destructive for them and anyone who works with them.

When I first started coaching Todd, he struggled with chronic stress and was easily triggered. He was lashing out at his team, and it was destroying morale. You could feel his impatience and agitation. Mistakes were called out in front of the entire team. In his mind it was an expedient method of ensuring that everyone learned the lesson from their error, but it was humiliating for the individual and instilled fear in his team.

When Todd wasn't stressed out, he was funny and likable. But those moments of losing his cool had taught people to stay on guard. Things had gotten so bad that his team had a private group chat that they used to monitor his mood from the moment he walked in the door, and the thread was always consulted to get a read on his mood before any one-on-one meetings.

After receiving some poor feedback, and unable to bear the constant stress anymore, Todd reached a point where he really wanted to change his leadership style. Over the next year, we worked to identify his triggers (mistakes, excuses, and missed deadlines), understand the beliefs and stories behind them, and recognize the physical warning signals. Then, using the quarter-second lag, he learned to intervene and change his response when he felt triggered. Over time, the turnaround in his behavior and stress level was remarkable. When he asked questions, his tone remained open and curious. When he needed to address performance issues, he calmly spoke to the employee outside of a team meeting. He worked hard to be consistent in his responses and build back trust—and it worked! His team started performing better, people were happier, and there was a genuine sense of collaboration that any company would admire. It took real effort, but as his consciousness increased, the impact that external influences had on him decreased.

We all have the ability to evolve and grow. And when we're able to use this split-second moment to our advantage, it can dramatically improve our relationships and well-being. We can reclaim control over how we respond and how we impact others. The more we understand what's driving us, the less power it has over our thoughts, emotions, and actions. We begin to realize that we have the ability to change our response and behave differently. And every time we change the way we do things, our brain will change as well.

CHANGING YOUR MIND

If you're like most people, somewhere along the path to understanding your communication style you'll discover something about the way you instinctually interact with people that you'd like to change. You may want to talk less and listen more, or learn to speak up when you disagree. The good news is that you *can* change. We all have the ability to change our minds—to evolve the way we think, alter what we do, and operate from a higher state of being. Granted, it takes a high level of self-awareness, positive intentions, and consistent practice, but changing how we communicate is completely within our reach. And it's worth it.

When you raise your level of expression, you lower your stress. This tends to inspire people to make even more changes to optimize the way they communicate. For example, when you learn to constructively address conflict rather than avoid it, you ultimately reduce interpersonal tension. When you learn to listen rather than always lead, you deepen relationships. And when you take responsibility for how you communicate, you build trust. Shifting out of deeply rooted behaviors may not feel easy, but it is possible. You can transform the way you're wired to habitually respond through a three-step process that empowers you to change your brain—one that moves you from thinking to doing to being.

Neuroscientists originally believed that once the brain was hardwired, we couldn't change how we operated; we simply were who were. Thankfully, it turns out that the brain's wiring is far more flexible than was thought, and we have the ability to reprogram the circuitry that directs our behavior. There's a part of the brain called the neocortex that's responsible for higher-order functions such as cognition, language, and spatial reasoning, and it's also the most malleable part of our brain.[9] Every time we learn something new—like when we read a book to learn a new language or to develop new skills to improve our communication— our neocortex is forming new synaptic connections.

As we learn, the brain's circuitry begins to fire in new sequences as it establishes new neural connections. This is what allows us to create new ways of thinking.[10] Once those pathways are established, we need to reinforce what we've learned to strengthen the bonds so they remain intact. Think of it like treading a new path: Every time we walk over the same ground, the more prominent the path becomes, and once we stop it begins to fade away. The same holds true for when we're learning something new. The more we think about an idea, concept, or approach, the stronger those connections become—and when we stop reinforcing the connections, they weaken.

Of course, knowledge alone won't change the way you think; you need to experience what you've learned. It's through lived experience that you begin to cement these new synaptic connections. Remember, the pathways that get used the most become your autopilot settings—so in order to change your ways of thinking and communicating, you need to blaze these new trails repeatedly and frequently. When we put ideas into action, we engage all five senses; they then relay a variety of input from different sensory pathways back to our brain, causing bundles of neurons to organize themselves around this new experience. These neurons produce chemicals that create feelings and engage the limbic system (emotions). This means that when we change our behavior and create a new experience, we link the mind and body—and now we have both our thinking and emotional brains working together to support the changes we're trying to make. Simply put, we need to put the ideas we learn into action if we want to change.

However, putting an idea into action just once isn't going to do it; it takes repeated effort. The brain's ability to rewire its autopilot programming is based upon the neuroscience principle that says *the nerve cells that fire together wire together*. When two neurons connect, they anchor a memory in your brain. The more we repeat our new behaviors, the faster the neurons fire and wire together. Ultimately, they form new neural networks filled with positive memories that become dominant and support behavioral change, skill development, and new habits.

Now, let me be clear: even a dozen experiences won't solidify change in the brain. We need to deepen the mind-body connection by repeating the behavior again and again (and again). The goal is to consciously embody our new behaviors, and this takes considerable energy and practice. To truly change our mindset or behaviors, we need to convert these active choices into automatic, subconscious responses—in other words, memories.

This process takes some time and the more experiences you have the faster you'll entrain the memories that create the change. It also takes some mental effort to change, because our new thoughts have to compete with well-established neural networks that have been repeatedly wired, sometimes for decades. But over time, as you put new ways of thinking into action, the new neural pathway will become the strongest and loudest in your head, and this becomes the program that runs the way you think, feel, and behave. When that circuit becomes the most dominant pathway—and your new memories are more powerful—the brain begins to wire it in more permanently. In order to prioritize this new pathway, your brain begins to quite literally prune memories of the old thoughts and behaviors.[11]

Let's look at an example of how these steps come together to dissolve a common emotional trigger: receiving feedback. Let's say you read a book on adopting a growth mindset to help you stop personalizing feedback. You learn new techniques to shift your perspective and spend hours thinking through the self-coaching tips. The repetition of thought has caused your neurons to fire and wire together so you're able to retrieve the ideas faster and faster.

The next time you're receiving feedback, you begin to feel your throat constrict as fear and self-doubt resurface. But now your brain automatically connects you to the self-coaching techniques you've learned. You tell yourself to breathe deeply, listen objectively, and hear the compliments too. The moment you begin to practice what you've learned your body begins to settle down and feel safe again. Your new behavior is creating a new experience and what your mind understood intellectually is now being felt throughout your body. You're embodying the knowledge and creating new memories to dissolve the wiring that held your fear of feedback in place.

Remember, a single experience isn't enough to replace the more dominant neural circuitry, but every time you receive (or seek!) feedback and apply the techniques you begin to neurologically hardwire the new circuitry in place. With enough repetition, your mind and body become aligned and begin operating on autopilot in ways that set you up for success.

• • •

The human mind has been brilliantly designed with the ability to evolve and change. It doesn't happen on its own, but as your self-awareness expands, you can gain control over the situations that trigger you and the negative programming that holds you back. You can learn to use the lag time—that split second between impulse and reaction—to choose how you respond and to override the early programming that no longer serves you. Granted, it takes time to erase the old stories you tell yourself. But they will gradually fade away as you have new experiences and rewrite the program to upgrade your operating system to one that allows you to communicate at your best more often.

CHAPTER 3

We're All Connected

*W*hile it may seem that we're separate, distinct entities, the reality is that we're all connected and communicating on multiple levels at all times. Now you might be thinking that this is a bunch of New Age nonsense, but breakthrough discoveries in quantum physics, a discipline that explains how everything in the universe works down to subatomic systems, has proven that there's far more than meets the eye.

Quantum physicists have been studying the fabric of the universe for over seventy years, and one of their most important—and more recent—discoveries is that everything in our world is connected to everything else through an intelligent field of energy called the quantum field or the zero-point field. Our consciousness plays an integral role in everything that we experience every day. If thoughts equal energy and energy equals matter, then thoughts become matter. And our thoughts have creative properties. In other words, life isn't happening *to* us, life is happening *because* of us.[1]

On a macro level, the quantum field keeps us all connected. On a micro level, each of us has a personal energy field that surrounds us because the human body is electromagnetic. Our individual energy field is always connected to the quantum field—on an atomic level, we're interconnected with everyone and everything. These energy fields are in constant communication, sending and receiving information. Studies have shown that these invisible energy fields communicate through frequencies and vibrations, and they carry information between us that influences how we think, feel, and behave.

Whether we're aware of it or not, we're always communicating on an energetic level. We pick up on the "vibe" in the room—something just doesn't "feel right" or you might have a "funny feeling" that puts you on alert. Typically, we chalk it up to gut instinct or intuition when what we're really tapping into are the energy fields that are surrounding us and transmitting information. When you understand how this works, you can learn to communicate from a higher level of consciousness to create more positive and trusted relationships through your thoughts, intentions, and emotions.

Anecdotally, we've all experienced energetic communication. Have you ever found yourself thinking of someone and then they call or text you? Or maybe you've been in a meeting where someone says exactly what you were thinking before you could get the words out? Our thoughts, intentions, and emotions all carry frequencies that radiate into the world, especially toward the people we're closely connected to. It also means that we can consciously use our interconnectivity to elevate the way we communicate and shape our interpersonal experiences.

This intelligent energy field is meant to keep us all connected, so that we're better able to understand and support one another. Our true nature is to be kind, compassionate, and cooperative. But we've been taught to be competitive and look out for our own self-interest through centuries of conditioning. The principle of "survival of the fittest" became the foundation around which our societies and economies have been built. Darwin's original idea of natural selection led to this evolutionary theory, but when you read *The Descent of Man* it's easy to see how distorted it all became. Darwin writes about "survival of the fittest" only 2 times, but he writes 95 times of love; he writes 12 times of selfishness, but 92 times of moral sensitivity (compassion); and 9 times of competition but 24 times of mutual aid (cooperation). He argued that the success of human evolution is tied to our compassion and concern about the well-being of others that extends to both strangers and all sentient beings.[2] Darwin explained more than a century ago that we're at our best when we work collaboratively, empathize, and look out for one another—an assertion that has long been supported by anthropologists and sociologists. And today, this idea is finally rising within us and leading to the evolution of conscious companies.

Many of us grew up in "sink or swim" work environments under leadership that instilled a sense of fear and competition, where quarterly earnings and shareholder value led every decision. Today, many businesses, employees, customers, and investors have woken up to the fact that this approach isn't sustainable or healthy. We're at an inflection point as the business paradigm is changing and cultures are being designed around purpose, employee well-being, and creating a positive impact. We can all play a pivotal role in accelerating the changes we want to experience in our work and in our world. Cultures are made up of people—that's us! And when we intentionally change how we connect with one another, we're well on our way to creating the change we want to see in the world.

WE'RE ALWAYS BROADCASTING AND RECEIVING INFORMATION

Most of us tend to think of communication purely in terms of the words, tone, gestures, and facial expressions we use to get our message across, but as you're beginning to understand it's so much more than that. There's a whole communication system that operates just below our conscious level of awareness that's always sending and receiving messages between us; it operates on an electromagnetic (or "energetic") level that's subtle and yet highly influential. Every thought, intention, and emotion carries a frequency that moves through this field of energy. This means that you're always sending messages to others—messages that you may not even be aware of—that influence how they feel, think, and behave, and vice versa.

The energy fields that surround our bodies are highly active and perceptive. The brain and the heart generate rhythmic electromagnetic fields of energy that telegraph what we're thinking and feeling. You might think that the brain would be more powerful in sending out energetic signals, but the heart's field is actually much larger and more powerful—it's about 100 times stronger. In fact, the heart's field can be detected several feet outside the body in all directions with sensitive magnetometers. This magnetic field is why we're able to "feel" other people's emotions.[3] It's an innate ability that we all possess that heightens our awareness around what others are going through and it allows us to feel empathy.

Some of the most powerful messages we send are delivered energetically. We've all been in conversations where we sense that something isn't quite right; we pick up on a signal and just know something is off. We've also been in conversations where we can feel that people are genuine, caring, and honest; it's why you can have a deep sense of trust with someone you've only just met. What you're sensing is the energetic vibration of the other person—you're feeling and experiencing their thoughts, intentions, and emotions through the exchange that happens between your energy fields.

PEOPLE CAN FEEL YOUR INTENTIONS

Our intentions also send an energetic message about what's really driving what we say and do, and what we don't say or do. Even when *you* may not be consciously aware of what's motivating you, people can sense your intentions. Studies have shown that the heart and brain are linked to the quantum field; they quite literally pick up the vibrational frequency of our intentions and bring them into people's awareness. Consciousness research has even demonstrated that through this process people can accurately discern truth from lies.[4] This means people can feel when your intentions are pure and positive or deceptive and manipulative.

While the way energy communicates is pretty straightforward, the way people communicate is not. When we distrust someone's motives, we typically don't let on. We don't say "I feel like you're lying to me" or "I feel like you're trying to manipulate me." We play along and act like everything is fine. We all do it, but that doesn't mean we ignore or forget what we've picked up on. It erodes trust. And, in the future, we keep our guard up and question their motives. Sometimes we understand that what we're feeling are the "little white lies" we've all told to avoid dealing with things head-on. Like when your boss or a colleague checks in on a project and you say "I'm working on that right now!" when you haven't even started. Other times they're much larger issues, like when someone takes credit for an idea that wasn't theirs. The point is people can feel your intentions even when they act like they don't. This is why it's always a good idea to be open and honest. It may not feel easier in the moment, but it's easier in the long run.

When you're operating under stress, it's even more important to stay connected to your intentions. Work pressure has a way of bringing out expedient behaviors that can damage relationships. We tend to push, or tell half-truths, when we're trying to move things along and get people on board. We rationalize and justify what we feel are necessary measures, but the reality is that when we communicate on this level it damages our relationships.

Intentions are pretty easy to spot when you take the time to look. They're often right at the surface and tied to our level of awareness and well-being. The more conscious you become of your intentions, the faster you'll learn to recognize what's really motivating you. And over time, you'll begin to see your intentions as they're taking shape. You'll hear the thoughts in your mind and feel the emotions in your body that clearly signal your motives. When you reach this level, you're able to consciously redirect any self-serving intentions and choose to elevate the way you engage.

When we're well-intentioned, we can positively direct all forms of communication to create more optimal outcomes. When the depth of this truth sinks in, you begin to appreciate how important it is to hold a positive intention at all times.

EMOTIONS ARE CONTAGIOUS

Have you ever been in a meeting where someone arrives in a great mood and you can feel their happiness light up the room? Or, on the flip side, have you ever noticed how one person's bad mood can infect an entire team and pull them into a downward spiral? Scientists call this phenomenon *emotional contagion*, which means that one person's emotions and behaviors trigger similar emotions and behaviors in others. Many studies have shown that when teams are exposed to emotional contagion their behavior shifts. When groups experience positive emotions, they work together more effectively—performance goes up and conflict goes down. People are naturally more open and collaborative, and they work together to make decisions more equitably. The antithesis was also true: when negative emotions infect groups, tensions rise and productivity drops as people put their own needs over those of others. While these findings may not seem all that surprising, what *is* interesting is that teams were completely unaware that emotions were driving their behavior.[5]

Our emotions play a significant role in how people respond to us. We all have the ability to be a catalyst and spread positive emotions and it can be as simple as smiling, using eye contact, and open body language to influence how people feel. Thanks to the mirror neurons in our brain, we naturally mimic the social behaviors of others. When scientists discovered that mirror neurons fire in the same pattern whether we're performing an action or simply watching it, it was a huge breakthrough in understanding why and how behaviors and emotions spread through groups. By simply observing someone's behavior our minds and bodies are signaled to re-create the same response.[6] It's why we naturally smile back when someone smiles at us and why we frown when we see someone is unhappy. We're wired to share and feel what others are going through. These principles hold true whether we're talking to one person, a team, or presenting to an audience—we influence one another all the time.

WE INFLUENCE OUR EXPERIENCES

When you understand how your energy—meaning your thoughts, intentions, and emotions—affects the way people respond to you, it becomes obvious that you significantly influence the experiences you have with people. Learning to consciously direct your energy is one of the keys to elevating your level of communication. And the better we know ourselves, the more empowered we are to create on this level. This is why it's so important to understand your communication style; it connects you to insights that help you see yourself more clearly. It's also important to stay aware of your physical, emotional, and mental states—well-being—since they directly impact how we communicate.

When you're feeling healthy, happy, and confident you broadcast positive thoughts and emotions like appreciation, compassion, acceptance, empathy, and joy. You're in a creative mode, sending out energy that carries a high vibration and frequency that uplifts people. At the opposite end of the spectrum is survival mode: when we're feeling tired, under pressure, and overwhelmed. Our stress hormones kick in and create thoughts and emotions around fear, frustration, competition, insecurity, anxiety, and shame. These emotions carry a very low energy, frequency, and vibration that pull everyone else down.[7] The good news is that when you change your mood you change your stress response. And that begins to change everything.

We have the ability to deliberately generate positive emotions to change our mood, thoughts, and energy. In Part 3, you'll learn a number of proven techniques to elevate your emotions. Once we begin to generate heartfelt emotions, the magnetic field generated by the heart expands its vibration and connects us to the quantum field. Our vibration now carries the frequency of our positive emotions and this energy becomes the signature of our energetic communication.

Our profound interconnectedness gives us even more opportunities to transform how we communicate. We have the ability to use this connection to build healthy working relationships through pure intentions, positive emotions, and genuine listening. When you're operating on this level, you'll be at your best more often than not.

CHAPTER 4

Staying Tuned In

$\mathcal{T}$he irony of being a good communicator is that your ability to express yourself isn't the most important factor in the equation. Genuine listening is one way to elevate your communication skills. It's impossible to be a great communicator if we don't listen to each other. How well you listen has a major impact on the quality of your relationships and how effective you are at your job. Listening is key to being able to understand information as well as people. It's how you build rapport and show you care. And it's foundational for building trust.

Everyone wants to feel heard, but most of us would rather be talking than listening. When we're talking, we feel more in control; we get to steer the conversation where we want it to go and we don't have to discuss topics we have zero interest in. Plus, when we're talking the focus is on us, so we're not bored. But the problem with this approach is that when conversations are replaced by personal broadcasting, we lose our ability to connect with one another.

Communication is an *exchange* of ideas and information. Human connection requires a balance between talking and listening, and somewhere along the way we've lost that balance. Perhaps it's because the predominant forms of communication in our work cultures are meetings and emails, where there's little room for true dialogue and real-time listening, which causes many to tune out and reply without deep listening. But what if we were to improve our communication skills and make every conversation matter? What if we placed a premium on building trusted working relationships? Well, for one thing, we'd have fewer misunderstandings. We'd also be more productive and experience less stress. And just imagine how much shorter meetings would be if we were all engaged—listening more and talking less. It's not as hard as you think, and the upside is huge.

Improving communication improves everything. And if you want to become a better communicator you need to become a better listener. Real listening is rare—it requires our full attention, patience, and empathy. You learn to read between the lines, so you hear what's said and unsaid. Part of what gets in our way is that we think we're better listeners than we are. We think listening is easy and natural. But it's not. Genuine listening is a skill that needs to be learned and practiced every day. It's like a muscle; the more you use it, the stronger it gets.

LISTENING IS HARD

You'd think that since listening is critical to communication, we'd be better at it. But listening is hard. To begin with, the brain can process information much faster than we can speak. The average person talks at about 225 words per minute, but we can listen at more than twice that rate—500 words per minute. The mind doesn't like the gap, so it begins to fill in those other 275 words per minute with our own thoughts.[1] Sure, we hear the words, but we're not actually focused on trying to understand their perspective; we're busy thinking about our own perspective and what we want to say. Have you ever found yourself in a conversation with someone and while they're still trying to get their point across you're already forming your response? Of course you have! We all do it. The brain is conditioned to start processing information as it flows in, so even if you start off with the intention of listening, it's difficult to maintain. Before we know it, we're distracted by our own thoughts: What do *I* think about this? Do *I* agree? Do *I* disagree? How should *I* respond? We become so focused on our own point of view we don't even notice that we're half listening at best.

Then there's the issue of how easily distracted we've all become. The Information Age has simultaneously given us an abundance of "shiny" things to focus on and narrowed our attention span.[2] We're used to being saturated with visual information, sound bites, and hyperlinks. Thanks to a never-ending stream of breaking news and what's trending on Twitter, discussions have become headlines and our attention fragments beyond 280 characters. We're used to communication that moves at warp speed. And by comparison, the pace of a meeting or conversation feels painfully slow. It takes real effort, energy, and patience to stay engaged.

While we have more ways to connect to one another, it actually makes it harder to listen. Just think about how difficult it is to stay focused on a conversation when an email, text, Slack message, or notification pops up. There's so much going on in our minds, and so many distractions, that we don't have the mental or emotional space to give someone our full attention. But we can learn to clear our minds, turn off the distractions, and create real connections that deepen our understanding and build trust.

DO YOU REALLY LISTEN?

You've probably already heard a lot of advice on how to show people that you're listening: make eye contact, match their body language, paraphrase what they say, smile and nod to show you're paying attention. Sure, these things give the illusion that you're listening, but these "strategies" have always seemed a bit artificial to me. Yes, you should look at someone when they're talking. But there's no need to *perform* to let someone know that you're listening if you are, in fact, listening. They can already tell.

That being said, listening is a skill and there are some practices you'll want to develop that will make it easier to stay tuned in. One of the quickest ways to become a better listener is to eliminate the distractions you can control. This means technology. Did you know that, subconsciously, when your phone is present, it's always demanding part of your attention? It turns out that the mere possibility that our phones may ring decreases our awareness and understanding when we're communicating by 20%.[3] This means that if we just leave our phones behind, or put them on airplane mode, we're already more present. The same goes for bringing your computer to a meeting. You can't take notes and also give someone your full attention. It might feel uncomfortable not having your phone or computer within reach—we've conflated being perpetually available with being good at our job. And you may feel disconnected if you're not always up to date on what's happening—a discomfort that has its roots in a powerful, evolutionary need for belonging and connectedness. But we aren't fully connecting with people when we fragment our attention.

Real listening requires being fully present. This means we need to stop multitasking while we're talking with people. The fact is no one is able to able to multitask, not even women. We might think we can do several things at once and do them well, but we can't. All we're doing is further fragmenting our attention. The problem is that multitasking has become so common that we've convinced ourselves that we're more effective when we juggle multiple things at once. Again, we're not. Here's proof. Research in neuroscience has shown repeatedly that the mind can focus only on one thing at a time; the brain cannot, I repeat, *cannot* do multiple tasks simultaneously. It just switches tasks quickly. Every time we move from one task to the next—from listening to answering a text to jotting down a note—there's a stop/start process that goes on in the brain. This process actually takes more time than if we were to give someone—or something—our full attention and focus. Not only is multitasking inefficient but it takes a toll on our performance and productivity. We tend to make more mistakes and use more energy.[4]

When you're using technology to connect—Zoom, FaceTime, phone calls—it's just as important to turn off any notifications that will pull your attention away from the conversation or meeting. We're often so overwhelmed by the sheer volume of information flowing in that we try to multitask while we're having a conversation. How many times have you been talking with someone, or on a Zoom call, and secretly been going through emails or responding to texts? We knowingly split our attention and trade real listening for an empty in-box.

But that's not all we're trading; we're also trading an opportunity to understand someone more fully and our chance to deepen trust. Remember, people can feel your intentions and they know when you're listening and when you're not—even if they don't say anything, they know. When you make it a practice to always close your email, apps, and notifications, you'll find it much easier to stay present, listen, and build trust.

This same principle holds true for mental multitasking. If you're in a conversation, be in the conversation. If you're in a meeting, be in the meeting. Don't start outlining a report in your head. Don't think about your to-do list. Or what you're going to make for dinner. Be present. The reality is that thoughts are always going to be flowing into your mind and there will be times you mentally drift away. Your job is to learn to recognize the mental chatter and bring your attention back. Just take a deep breath, smile because you noticed, and return to the conversation.

Practice Really Listening

- Set an intention to listen. This simple act will direct your mind to pay attention.
- Eliminate any technology you're not using. Close your apps. Turn off your phone. Shut your laptop if you can or maximize your video-call screen to mimic being "in the room" without distractions.
- Notice moments you drift away from the conversation (e.g., thinking about your next meeting, running through your to-do list, or planning dinner).
- If you notice that you've drifted, take a deep breath, smile, and bring your attention back to the discussion.
- Check in after your conversation and see how present you were. Were you able to stay tuned in? How many times did you have to pull your thoughts back?

When we make it a point to really listen to people, we build stronger relationships. Our level of trust deepens. And there's far less miscommunication.

HEARING WHAT ISN'T SAID

In nearly every conversation there are the overt messages being delivered, but there are also the subtle undertones that contribute crucial layers of subtext to the message. Most of us have some intuitive skills around how to read people, sense group dynamics, and assess different situations. We can usually recognize the signals that tell us the direction of a conversation by paying attention to word choice, tone, body language, and pacing, as well as how people are responding. A quick glance around the room will give you a feel for whether the situation is relaxed or if there's tension in the air. But then there are the more subtle signals—the unspoken dynamics that influence a conversation or meeting. That feeling you have in your gut that there's a hidden agenda when someone pushes a point. Or you may pick up on hints of stress and anxiety that are prompting someone to behave differently. People seldom directly express the more complex emotions or challenges they're concerned about. Instead, they quietly signal their motives, needs, and fears through body language, tone, pacing, or a remark that stands out. Listening on multiple levels fills in the gaps between what's said and what's left unsaid.

When you can see and understand other people—what they really want, what motivates them, what they may be afraid of, or what they may be hoping for—you learn to see what they need and what's driving the conversation. Reading people on this level requires that you stay tuned in and observe how they respond to you and others. You watch for projecting to make sure you're not misreading the situation. And you become adept at scanning the room for the nearly invisible cues that tell you what's really going on. These layers of information allow you to adapt and respond, so you can turn a good conversation into a great one—or turn around a challenging conversation when you sense things aren't going well.

The more you observe people and their reactions the faster you'll be able to read them, see group dynamics, and understand what's unfolding.

Practice Reading the Room

Put your own emotions aside. It's difficult to read another person's emotions if we're caught up in our own. If you're feeling emotional before you enter a meeting, take a few minutes to breathe deeply to calm your emotions and clear your mind. This will help you to come in feeling centered and attuned to the needs of others.

Observe the details. *Scan the room* when you walk in and regularly throughout the meeting to see what you pick up on. Note your first impression. What does it feel like? Keep an eye out for microexpressions like a raised eyebrow, a fleeting smile, or an eye roll.

Watch for interactions. How do people position themselves in the room? Do they sit close to others? Or create distance? Are there side conversations going on? Are people dialed in or tuned out?

Watch for emotional cues. Facial expressions often reveal how someone is feeling. Make a point to watch the speaker and regularly scan the faces of others in the room. Who looks happy? Who looks tense? Who is annoyed? Who's bored?

Listen with empathy. See if you can hear and understand the needs or concerns behind someone's emotion. Practice getting a sense for what people may be feeling but not saying.

Listen for tone. What's the emotion and intention behind a person's tone? It speaks volumes about what someone is saying or too uncomfortable to say.

Read body language. Watch for gestures, smiles, and nods. Are people leaning in or away? Are they engaged and sitting up? Or disengaged and slouching?

There's a big difference between hearing and listening. Listening requires being present, learning to trust your instincts, and discerning what people are really saying. Nonverbal communication can be just as powerful as what we say with our words. The more you intentionally listen to the subtle signals the more you'll pick up on, and the better you'll understand others.

EMPATHIC LISTENING CONNECTS US

We've all had really great conversations where you walk away feeling perfectly understood. You feel like you've made a real connection and you're inspired by what you've learned. This is what happens when people are present, open, and genuinely trying to understand each other. There's no reason why the majority of our interactions can't be like that. However, it does require that we work to listen with more empathy and understanding.

We may hear with our ears, but we listen with all of our senses. The best communicators use empathic listening to deepen interpersonal connections; they listen with the intention to stay open, curious, and watch for judgment. They give us the time we need to share our thoughts; there's no rushing the conversation or pushing of an agenda. When someone is sincerely listening with an open mind, you can feel it. It helps us feel safe. And when we feel safe, our defenses come down and we're genuine.

We all have the ability to cultivate more empathy. Our brains are actually wired to connect with others through an "empathy circuit" that naturally helps us to feel what others are feeling.[5] Our job is to learn how to tune in fully and listen with all of our senses. When we engage on this level, we're able to pick up on the subtle cues—language choice, tone, gestures, and body language. You listen for the person's underlying wants, needs, and emotions. You listen for what they believe and value. You learn to listen for the undercurrents that are filled with meaning. This allows us to understand and connect with people on a deeper level. It also tends to bring out our best qualities and make collaboration much easier.

The more you practice showing empathy the easier it gets and the more it spreads; it turns out that empathy is contagious. Studies have shown that when the group sees that it's normal to encourage openness and understanding, the entire team is more likely to show more empathy and humanity.[6] Clearly, this bodes well for collaboration and building healthy teams.

Practice Listening with Empathy

Empathy is a skill that can be developed. You learn to set aside your viewpoints and practice seeing things through another person's perspective. It can be difficult to empathize with people you don't enjoy, but if you're willing to try, you'll find that your relationship has a much better chance of improving. There are a number of techniques you can use to cultivate more empathy for others. Practice applying a few at a time to expand and strengthen this muscle.

Prepare to listen. Take a few minutes to clear your mind, quiet your emotions, and become aware of anything that may get in the way of your ability to listen with an open mind. Turn off your notifications and put away any devices or distractions.

Set an intention. You might choose to stay engaged, quiet mental chatter, remain open, be curious, or watch for judgment.

Engage your intuition. Listen to your gut instincts to read between the lines. Pay attention to what's said *and* what goes unsaid. What needs, beliefs, or values are you hearing or sensing?

Listen for tone, pacing, and language. Do they sound calm or more stressed? Does it feel relaxed or is there an urgency? Are they speaking in absolutes? Or is it an open discussion?

Keep your body language open. Use your body language to let others know you're listening: make eye contact, use friendly facial expressions, keep your body open and turned toward them.

Let people finish. Good listeners rarely interrupt! They wait for the speaker to signal that they're done before sharing their thoughts or asking a question.

Acknowledge their position. Whether you agree with someone or not, let them know that you understood their perspective and feelings around the topic at hand. Acknowledge what they've shared and empathize in a way that makes them feel heard.

When we show more empathy, we create an opening for more meaningful conversations where people are authentic. We begin to understand people better. And when we understand one another, it's less likely that there will be miscommunication or misunderstandings that fuel unnecessary tension and stress. More important, when we understand and trust one another, we can work together and use our collective talents to create a positive impact in the world.

Part 2

Communication Styles

CHAPTER 5

Understanding the
Communication Styles

*H*umankind is instilled with an innate desire for self-knowledge and self-understanding. We have an intrinsic need to learn and grow, and we've been on this path of self-exploration for thousands of years. This concept of "know thyself" has enthralled philosophers since the days of Socrates, Plato, and Aristotle. They believed that the acquisition of wisdom that comes from "knowing one's Self" is ultimately what allows us to grow and evolve and care for the well-being of society. This belief has inspired countless generations to expand their level of conscious awareness and led us to a point in time where the areas of personal growth and well-being are now a part of business training programs.

We all have different styles, personalities, and strengths, which are as unique to us as our fingerprints. These characteristics often make it more difficult for us to work well with some people. It's well understood that people problems are often the most challenging, stressful, and emotionally draining issues we face at work. In part, it's because we all have our own ways of doing things that work well for us, but *our* ways don't always work as well for others.

If you've been in the workplace for any length of time, you know that your technical skills will only carry you so far. You may be an exceptional architect, accountant, or product manager, but if you can't communicate effectively and get along well with the people you work with, your success will be limited. Conversely, people who develop their communication and interpersonal skills seem to thrive in any environment. This is why it's so important to know and understand yourself—and to know and understand others.

STYLES PROVIDE PERSONAL INSIGHTS

Communication styles give us a framework for gaining a deeper understanding of Self; they make it easier to see our talents as well as our patterns of behavior that are often invisible to us. Our most ingrained patterns tend to live on a subconscious level, in the programming that drives the way we think, feel, and act. Through our style reflections we can access new levels of personal insight that support our growth and help us to see how to work well with other styles. It's essential that we understand who we are and what drives us if we want to make meaningful improvements to how we communicate and develop new skills.

Carl Jung, who founded the field of analytical psychology in the early twentieth century, was one of the first to develop the idea of personality types and explore how they influenced our relationship with the world and each other.[1] He could see that while all human beings are unique, we also have many shared qualities that bridge the gaps created by our differences. Those shared qualities can be grouped into styles or types that provide general characteristics and traits that help your mind simplify the complexities of our individual nature.

Jung's groundbreaking model led to the creation of the DISC and Myers-Briggs personality style assessments and paved the way for our cultural obsession with self-discovery and climbing Maslow's hierarchy of needs toward self-actualization. If there's anything we know for sure it's that we all want to better understand and know ourselves. We're drawn to anything that helps us gain personal insights and access our full potential—from lighthearted Buzzfeed quizzes to the depths of Gallup's CliftonStrengths test. And as much as we want to understand ourselves, we also want to understand others. Knowing someone else's "type" can help us get a broad picture of their needs, motivations, tendencies, and preferences, which can help us see people more clearly.

In fact, many organizations use personality assessments to better understand their employees' style preferences, talents, and attitudes—and to help teams better understand one another—especially when it comes to how they interact socially. In my work as a consultant, I regularly used assessments to raise self-awareness, strengthen interpersonal connections, and give teams a common language to talk about their talents, needs, and preferences. A style model can be incredibly valuable, since we're surprisingly predictable, particularly when it comes to the way we communicate at work.

What's fascinating about human behavior is that the way we communicate in our professional lives is often quite different from how we behave in our personal lives. I've had clients who are very agreeable at work describe how they're practically tyrants at home. On the flip side, I've seen others who are domineering at work be easygoing around friends. Some people who are extremely inconsiderate to their colleagues display high levels of empathy with their family. We play different roles and engage in different ways in every aspect of our lives, which is why it's so important to understand how we show up at work.

Each of us has our own unique ways of communicating, with preferences that influence how we think, engage, manage stress, make decisions, use time, handle emotions, and deal with conflict. The irony is that what we struggle to see about ourselves is readily apparent to those around us. Most of us can describe in detail how our colleagues communicate and impact everyone around them, yet we're often blind to our own behaviors and habits. When you live within the texture of a pattern for so long it begins to fade away into the background; it's simply who you are and how you behave, and your style becomes practically invisible to you.

After years of coaching and consulting, I've seen the impact—both positive and negative—that one person's communication style can have on an organization, from a team level all the way to the boardroom. How we interact with one another at work powerfully influences an organization's culture. When we take responsibility for how we communicate, we create environments where people enjoy coming into the office and where they're capable of doing their best work. And in order to take responsibility for how we interact, we have to be able to accurately see ourselves. Therein lies the problem and the opportunity.

We all have blind spots around how we communicate and impact others. I've found that developing communication skills is *the* most effective path to building trusted working relationships and conscious cultures. What I couldn't find was a solid communication style assessment tool with profiles that supported personal development and interpersonal understanding. I wanted a tool that went beyond the surface so people could really understand how they communicate; one that would allow you to learn to master your style, reduce stress, and build trust so you can have a positive impact in everything you do. So I set out to create one.

COMMUNICATION STYLES ARE LIKE CONSTELLATIONS

If you've ever taken a personality assessment, you're probably quite familiar with the quadrant approach to defining different styles. This approach places you in one of four categories, with the lines clearly drawn, and each style equal in size. I've used several tools with this design with my clients, and while there were always aspects of a given tool that felt spot-on, each had its limitations and was incomplete when it came to describing how people communicate. For one thing, the variety of dimensions that influence how we communicate at work—such as how well we collaborate, our comfort level in challenging authority, or how willing we are to take risks—is simply too complex to place us in a tidy box. When I see models where the styles fall neatly into quadrants with equal populations, my experience tells me that these outcomes have more to do with research design than the possibility that we live in an orderly world. To put it simply, we aren't squares. We're constellations.

What my team and I learned after fielding an in-depth quantitative research study was that there are four unique communication styles, each one a constellation made up of distinct clusters of habitual behaviors across the three dimensions of assertiveness, collaboration, and consideration.

The assertiveness cluster of behaviors center around how forceful or direct you are in the way you communicate. It considers how you handle conflict, deal with your boss, express emotions and opinions, and deliver information. The collaborative dimension speaks to how you like to engage with people at work. It looks at behaviors around individual or team working preferences, the level of interest you show in the lives of your coworkers, and how you build relationships. The consideration dimension focuses on how you behave when communicating with others. It measures aspects like whether you're deliberate or spontaneous, critical or supportive, serious or lighthearted. The composite of clustered behaviors across these three dimensions form the constellations that shape your shining qualities and inform each of the styles.

THE FOUR COMMUNICATION STYLES

Over the course of our research, we explored each of the four constellations that make up the communication styles: expressive, reserved, direct, and harmonious—each style comprising its own combination of defining characteristics, behaviors, and attitudes. For example, expressive and harmonious styles are both collaborative but differ dramatically when it comes to their tendency toward assertiveness. The Expressives are the largest group (37%), followed by Reserved (25%), Direct (22%), and Harmonious (16%).

Remember, just because some styles represent larger portions of the population than others there's no style that's better than another. They're just different. Each style has its strengths and weaknesses, skills and vulnerabilities. And, as is so often the case, our greatest strengths can quickly become our greatest weaknesses when taken to extremes. No matter your style constellation, leaning into its unique qualities will support you in creating a successful and fulfilling career.

Your communication style profile provides insights into what drives you, how you engage, and how you impact others. Knowing your style's strengths and weaknesses, its potential and its limitations, as well as areas of cooperation and friction with other styles, will help guide the way you communicate and think about communication. These insights into your style and those of others allow you to move through challenging conversations with more ease, similar to the way buoys mark a channel and help you navigate around hidden rocks and shallow waters.

Now, if there's one thing more complex than communication, it's people. There are far too many layers to who we are and how we interact to be defined by a single style. For this reason, you'll find that you have both a primary and secondary style. Your primary style dominates the way you communicate at work and your secondary style shows up to varying degrees, depending on the situation, who you're talking to, and the level of stress you're feeling. Some people feel everything in their secondary profile describes them, while others find that there are only a handful of traits that fit how they see themselves. You're in charge of deciding what resonates in each profile, so take what feels accurate and leave the rest behind.

While no communication style profile will ever fully capture the essence of an individual, they paint a very good picture of how people interact at work. They help you to recognize where you communicate well and where you need to improve. And they give you a foundation of self-awareness and personal insight that you can build on as you learn to play to your strengths, minimize conflict, and build trusted relationships.

THE STYLE EXPRESSIONS

Every style has a range of expressions that's influenced by our level of self-awareness, stress, and well-being. For example, you may have a style that excels at collaboration and enjoys dialogue, but when you're stressed or on deadline, you dominate conversations to keep the ball rolling. Or maybe your tendency to keep your personal and work lives separate transforms into perceptible impatience or coldness toward your colleagues when you aren't well rested and want to be left alone to focus on your work. Our levels of self-awareness, stress, and well-being fluctuate constantly, which means that how we express our style is equally dynamic.

Our behaviors shift back and forth between three primary operating modes: in health, on autopilot, and under stress. When you communicate from the **healthy** expression of your style, you're exceptionally effective in all forms of communication and with all kinds of people. You play to your strengths and deliberately manage around weaknesses, while flexing to meet the communication needs of others to put them at ease. Operating from the healthy expression of your style is the ultimate goal, but you can't live here permanently. Communicating in health is like accessing flow states—you intentionally engage and give people your full attention. When you hit that zone, your connections and performance are enhanced, and you feel energized by the exchange.

Autopilot describes the way you predominantly engage, day in and day out. When you communicate on autopilot, the subconscious mind is in control and your beliefs and habits direct how you interact. Every style has patterns of communication that are effective and others that are likely to create tension. When you have cultivated strong communication skills your patterns support you—you actively listen, stay open, and genuinely respond; this allows you to operate on autopilot quite successfully. But if your communication skills are less developed or you have destructive patterns, like unconsciously dominating conversations, avoiding conflict, or personalizing input, you're more likely to experience interpersonal issues accompanied by distress. Your level of well-being often plays a pivotal role in how you automatically respond. When you're feeling energized, emotionally stable, and inspired, you'll be far more effective on autopilot. And when you're tired, stressed, and emotionally frayed, it's a struggle to engage and respond well.

No style handles excessive stress particularly well. Our **stressed** style-based behaviors come out when we experience prolonged pressure and our level of well-being is low. Stress pushes us into extremes that—to put it mildly—don't bring out the best in us. We put our needs first and disregard others in order to make our way through a difficult situation or to get the work done. Sometimes we're unaware of the impact that our expedient behaviors have on people. And other times, we can clearly see how we're affecting people, but we justify our approach because of the strain we're under.

It goes almost without saying that we want to operate from a place of health as often as we can, and the critical factor in shifting between these three modes is our level of conscious awareness. Conscious awareness speaks to how well we understand ourselves and how mindful we are of our behavior in different situations. If we have a high level of conscious awareness, we can communicate far more effectively—even when our well-being is low and we're feeling stressed.

Conscious awareness means we can recognize when we're being judgmental or avoiding responsibility and choose to shift our behavior. And more important, we're able to use that critical, quarter-second lag time when we get emotionally triggered. We sense our body's alarm signals, and we know to take slow, deep breaths to calm the mind and body so we can intentionally choose how we respond.

Now, this is not to say that well-being doesn't matter—it matters a lot! Without that foundation of physical, emotional, and mental well-being we struggle to access the level of conscious awareness we need to communicate from a healthy expression. But when our conscious awareness is low, even the highest level of well-being can't save us from ourselves. We're practically blind to our reactions and impact on others. For example, I once had a colleague, Sarah, who came into a meeting clearly happy and carefree, but when the discussion turned to the decisions she'd made on a project she was leading, her entire demeanor changed. Her tone became defensive, she started making excuses and blaming colleagues—willing to throw anyone under the bus to save herself. She was oblivious to people's body language, clearly telegraphing disapproval and frustration toward how she was reacting. This incident cost her the trust of several of her colleagues, which she never fully recovered.

Your level of conscious awareness has the ability to carry you through those times when you're feeling stressed. The ideal is to cultivate high levels of both conscious awareness *and* well-being, so you can communicate from the healthiest expression of your style more often than not. The communication style profiles in the next chapter are designed to help you to more accurately see and reflect on how you communicate at work. Getting to know your style is the first step in the journey toward self-awareness.

Take the Assessment

We have created an online assessment that makes it easy to identify how you communicate at work. The Communication Style Assessment connects you to your primary and secondary styles using a proprietary algorithm that discerns how you express yourself at work. It was developed using a discriminant function analysis that accurately classifies your style using multiple dimensions of communication.

If you haven't already done so, complete the Communication Style Assessment at TheElevatedCommunicator.com. It's best to take the assessment when your energy is strong and you're feeling open. This will put you in a good mindset for thoughtfully reflecting on how you communicate, what your predominant behaviors are, and how you typically engage with others at work. We're able to see ourselves more objectively when we're feeling positive and we're much more critical of ourselves when we're feeling down. So, try not to take the assessment after a particularly stressful day or challenging conversation that has you riled up.

Once you complete the assessment and have received your primary and secondary styles, dive into the next chapter to see what resonates. I encourage you to begin with your own styles and then read through the other two to get the full picture. You'll quickly see what makes each style unique.

CHAPTER 6

Meet Your Communication Style

*I*dentifying your communication style is the first step toward better understanding how you naturally express yourself at work. Once you've taken the assessment at TheElevatedCommunicator.com, your profile will help you gain more personal insights into your strengths and the benefits of how you engage. You'll learn to recognize what people with different styles need out of a conversation, so you can intentionally build trusted working relationships that make work feel easier and more enjoyable. And you'll begin to see how your level of well-being affects the way you communicate and how, in turn, the way you communicate affects your well-being.

Again, your primary style reflects your dominant approach to how you communicate at work. This style profile will capture the majority of your communication attitudes, behaviors, and preferences. Your secondary style provides an overlay of communication traits that add more dimension to the way you interact with others. The combination of the two style profiles will help you discover your unique blend of communication talents.

In the next pages there are detailed descriptions of each communication style profile. They're easy to understand and absorb. Start by reading through your primary style and then move on to your secondary one. It's strongly recommended that you read through *all* the styles so you can better understand the full scope of expressions.

Remember, self-assessments aren't an exact science. They rely on a person's ability to be self-aware and objective when evaluating how they communicate most often at work—and most people aren't as self-aware as they believe they are. The results can also be influenced by a person's mood or if they answered questions based on how they wish they operated. We all have images of how we want others to see us and sometimes those images bend our perception of reality. After reading all the descriptions most people can tell if there's a style profile that more accurately reflects how they show up.

If you're wondering whether you've accurately identified your communication habits, read through all the descriptions to see which best represents the way you show up most often. Another alternative is to ask someone at work that knows you well—or maybe even a few people—to take the assessment on your behalf. This will give you a good sense of how you come across to others. But keep in mind that it doesn't factor in your internal dialogue, which shapes the communication behavior they see externally. For example, you may prefer to make decisions independently but recognize that a collaborative approach works better for the team, and so you override your preference. This could skew the results if people didn't understand that your behavior was more intentional and less instinctual.

As you're reading through your primary communication style, capture the words and phrases that best describe you on a piece of paper or in a journal. Writing them down will help to anchor the behavioral qualities you identify with most. Then move on to your secondary style and do the same. What rings truest for you? The combination of the two styles will help you to see how your communication constellation takes shape.

Pay attention to any memories or situations that come to mind as you're reading through your profiles and jot them down. The subconscious mind often surfaces past experiences that can help you see how your style comes to life. Listen to your inner dialogue as well. The words you say to yourself as you're reading your descriptions ("Oh man, that's so me!") often hold valuable insights.

A Note on Secondary Styles

Each profile includes some of the most common influences that a secondary style brings when paired with the primary style. It gives you a glimpse into how the styles work together most often. It's highly recommended that you read through your entire secondary style profile so you can see exactly what aspects ring true. Some people find that the entire description fits, while others feel they're a strong blend of their two styles, and still more find that only a few traits of their secondary style resonate.

EXPRESSIVE

Collaborative · Open · Assertive · Perceptive · Curious

Expressives are the most open, talkative, and outgoing of all the styles. As the largest style group (37%), they excel at bringing people together and making work more enjoyable. Establishing a personal connection drives the way they engage and allows them to build close working relationships and extensive networks. Communication comes easily and effortlessly to an Expressive. They're articulate and speak quickly; they like to keep the pace moving. They love to share their ideas and perspectives about everything. They're the quintessential "open book." It's important to them that people understand where they're coming from, and when their transparency is coupled with authenticity they quickly build trust.

Their innate ability to connect makes them natural collaborators; they're happiest working in teams, sharing ideas, and problem solving. They're high-energy people; they have the ability to light up a room and infuse life into a conversation or meeting. They like to make work more fun, which can steer conversations off track. When they become bored they're likely to strike up a side conversation, unaware that it can be distracting to others.

They openly share their emotions and opinions, and they value the same from others. They're curious about everyone's views and perspectives and often ask a lot of questions in an effort to genuinely understand their coworkers' perspectives and motivations. Expressives like to have a full picture of how people think and feel.

By the same token, they care about the personal lives of their coworkers. They enjoy hearing people's stories and ask questions to extract details—this helps them see the person behind the words. They listen for unexpressed questions and concerns. And while they enjoy discussions, they'll rein in conversations that have wandered too far. Skilled at reading the room, they know when it's time to move on and advance the work.

They gravitate toward leadership roles and are talented at defusing tension. They speak their mind and are comfortable challenging others, even their boss, when needed. For them, it's about finding the fastest path to addressing issues, resolving conflicts, and moving forward. They have a knack for injecting humor to lighten the mood when tension builds, and they feel most successful when their team is working well together.

They're verbal processors and often like to think out loud. Giving voice to their thoughts provides an opportunity to test-drive early concepts and see how others respond. They enjoy sharing new ideas to see what sparks through conversation, though at times this can make it difficult to stick to the agenda and stay on track.

Listening requires some restraint on their part, and most Expressive types think they're better listeners than they are. Their desire to share every idea that comes to mind combined with their near-constant reading of the room splits their attention. Attentively listening is a key way they show others that they respect and value their contributions, but it's a skill they must actively cultivate. They ask more questions than any other style; this helps them clarify and deepen their understanding.

Expressives enjoy working on highly productive teams. They themselves inspire creativity and productivity, managing to come to any discussion with their opinions formed yet able to keep an open mind. They value considering other viewpoints when making decisions. And they're willing to move forward even if everyone isn't on board.

Storytelling is their forte. They love to bring ideas to life with colorful language, imagery, examples, and metaphors. They choose their words with care and strike the right tone, knowing that words have the power to move people. Their enthusiasm is palpable, contagious, and magnetic. This draws people in when shared at the right time and place. It can also frustrate those with a Direct style, who are motivated by staying on task and keeping meetings brief.

An Expressive likes structured meetings and agendas, but will take a few detours to keep things interesting. They tend to use the most airtime and often dominate the conversation when they're not self-aware. If the conversation stalls, they'll quickly jump in. Conversations energize them and they can easily lose track of time, which causes them to frequently be running behind. However, when they're feeling the pressure of a deadline, they naturally pull back on the depth of their conversations and stick to business.

Strengths	Weaknesses
• Articulate, comfortable communicating	• Poor listener, dominates the conversation
• Quick pace, high energy, passionate	• Impatient, overpowering, speaks too quickly
• Defuses tension and conflict	• Can be intimidating, others shut down
• Ability to read people and room dynamics	• Personalizes and projects when reading the room
• Easygoing, fun, uplifts others	• Disruptive and distracting

STYLE EXPRESSIONS

When Expressives communicate from the *healthy* side of their style, they're at their best and can use their natural charm to build new connections and deepen existing working relationships. They listen with an attentiveness that makes people feel heard, and intentionally speak less so that quieter voices can find an opening and join the discussion. While they're quite confident in their opinions, they don't push to persuade or try to get people to fall in line. Instead, they'll seek out other perspectives to gain new insights. They genuinely want to hear what others are thinking and feeling so they can make informed decisions. When an Expressive intentionally communicates they gracefully facilitate conversations where people openly share ideas and problem-solve. Their authenticity builds trust, and their natural energy makes work more enjoyable.

On the other hand, when they're *stressed* and the pressure is on and deadlines are looming, Expressives tend to manipulate and push to get their way. You can almost feel the undercurrents pulling you in their direction, as they exert their influence and leave little room for discussion. Their pacing and tone make it clear that there's no time for deliberation. They jump in and cut people off, failing to listen to other ideas. Their expedient approach may get the work out the door, but it comes at a price. Few forget how forceful their nature can be, and they become suspect of their motives when this pattern persists.

Healthy-to-Stressed	
Build strong, trusted relationships; draw people into the conversation and put them at ease	Keep to themselves and are a bit more exclusive in their contact with people
Thoughtfully share their ideas and emotions, without pressure so there's room for disagreement and differing perspectives	Push opinions and try to persuade others to advance their ideas; overshare
Build consensus, are open to new ideas and perspectives, and look to learn from others	Operate more independently, make decisions, and sell them in
Fully engaged; they listen patiently and ask questions to clarify	Don't listen, are impatient, interrupt, and direct the conversation to keep advancing
Authentic, intentionally choose their words, tone, and delivery to put others at ease	Sarcastic, tone is off-putting, and can become overly critical

SECONDARY STYLE INFLUENCES

Secondary—Reserved

An Expressive who has Reserved as their secondary may sound like a paradox, but they're actually quite complementary. The combination strengthens their ability to build a large professional network and cultivate strong working relationships. They gain more discernment around how to keep things professional, so they don't reveal too much or lean too heavily on emotion when sharing their ideas. They become subtler influencing and shaping outcomes.

Their friendly and easygoing nature allows them to quickly build rapport with people. People enjoy working with them and are more open to following their direction. This makes them more effective at leading and building strong teams. They're skilled at rallying people behind the work that needs to be done and staying on task.

Secondary—Direct

When Direct is the secondary style for an Expressive, it amplifies their natural ability to lead and succinctly express their point of view. These strengths help them to confidently lead discussions, address issues that need to be resolved, and come to agreement. Their brisk pace and command of the situation can also make them feel a bit more intimidating at times.

They gain many complementary communication skills that shore up some areas of weakness, especially when the pressure is on and time is running short. They'll limit any small talk and get down to business more quickly. They're capable of maintaining a high degree of focus that allows them to stay on task and complete the work on time. They're happy to provide recommendations—or make decisions on their own—to keep things moving.

Secondary—Harmonious

The Expressive and Harmonious styles share more characteristics than any other combination of styles. This pairing naturally enhances their ability to deeply connect, charm, and build relationships. They're both people-oriented, skilled at reading the room, seeing what people need, and keeping things light and interesting. They love to build personal relationships at work and let the conversations flow, while keeping things warm and friendly. They have the ability to put people at ease, get them to open up, and foster strong connections.

The Harmonious style complements and strengthens an Expressive by adding the balance they need in certain aspects of communication: their ability to listen improves, they create more room for others to join the conversation, and they become more patient. They also look for more opportunities to encourage and support others on the team.

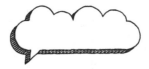

Expressive at a Glance

Communication Needs	Establish a personal connection
	Time to share and discuss ideas, Q & A
	Know that they have been heard
	Address disagreements without delay
Value	Creating an open and collaborative environment where teams share ideas, problem-solve, and work well together
Motivation	Being part of a connected team that succeeds
	Working together and openly sharing information
	Building consensus and advancing the work
Pace	Fast—they speak and respond quickly
Decision-Making	Collaborative—like to get everyone's input but will decide even if everyone isn't on board
Building Relationships	Makes a personal connection
	Openly shares their opinions and emotions
	Empathizes and asks questions
Managing Conflict	Steps in and addresses conflict

RESERVED

Confident · Connector · Private · Professional · Personable

People with a Reserved style are confident in their abilities and the most comfortable of all the styles in forming an opinion in the moment. This style represents 25% of the population and is known for fostering strong team connections. They have no problem speaking up. They actively participate in conversations and share their perspective. It's important to them that their voice is heard and that they influence the direction and outcome, but they don't dominate the conversation in order to get their point across, nor do they want to own the responsibility of making the final call.

In large part, their steady nature and the quality of their relationships add to their ability to be persuasive. Their delivery is very personable and always professional. They like to win others over while advancing their views; this makes them feel successful. This approach also fulfills their need to be both well-liked and influential.

Taking the lead holds little interest for them. They prefer to play a strong supporting role rather than sit at the helm; however, they do like to have a say in how the work advances. Known for being strong team players, they feel a sense of accomplishment when their work helps the team to advance and win. They take work fairly seriously and hearing that their contributions are valued goes a long way.

They expect everyone to work at their full capacity and support the team.

If they feel someone isn't pulling their weight, they'll address the issue in order to strengthen the team's performance. They step into the conversation that's needed, to ensure everyone is operating at their highest potential.

While Reserved types do place a high value on building and maintaining professional working relationships, they prefer to keep these relationships centered around their job. They need more privacy and may come across as a bit guarded since they don't reveal a lot about themselves or how they're feeling with a wide range of people. Instead, they like to form a few close friendships at work and keep the rest in a professional space. They don't like a lot of small talk or humor, preferring to stay focused on the work. They'll join in the conversation to build and maintain relationships, but you'll notice that Reserved types keep the conversation in a broad zone so things don't get too personal. People who are Direct really appreciate this about them. However, for the Harmonious and Expressive styles—who like to connect on a personal level and in a lighthearted way—Reserved types can come across as overly serious, cold, or aloof.

While others often respond in ways that have become expected, the Reserved style is less predictable. They see everything through the lens of the situation at hand. Context is crucial in determining their course of action. They steer from the middle using the current circumstances to shape their perspective and drive their response. They want to see both the big picture and a high level of detail; this gives them the level of information they need to feel confident when deciding which direction will guide their response and behavior.

They take a measured approach and weigh their options before choosing a path. There are times they step in to defuse tension and times when they sit back and watch things play out. They may get straight to the point or they may tell a story. How they show up is always contingent upon what they believe the conditions require of them. This deliberate and varied approach, coupled with their more private nature, can make it difficult for others to gauge how they'll respond.

The tempered demeanor of the Reserved style also comes through in their tone and pacing. They're known for being even-keeled and rarely get overly emotional during a conversation. There's a steadiness to them that's reassuring. It makes people feel safe and builds trust. They listen to different perspectives in order to learn, and factor them into how they position their recommendations.

Strengths	Weaknesses
• Confident, influential	• Avoid taking the lead, avoid responsibility
• Build strong professional relationships	• Guarded personally and a little distant
• Team player, provides constructive feedback	• Need to feel important, critical of others' performance
• Measured, thoughtful, and deliberate	• Risk-averse, too controlled, slow to decide
• Professional, stays on task	• Too serious, humorless

STYLE EXPRESSIONS

When a Reserved is operating from the *healthy* side of their style, they use their relationship skills to take the lead, advance the work, and help people feel like their contributions matter. They know how to foster a team spirit and get people to gel. And when they open up and lighten up a bit, they're even more effective. They share their perspective without trying to influence, and this puts people at ease. Others can feel that they're genuine, which helps to promote trust and create productive interactions.

However, when they're feeling overloaded and *stressed*, Reserveds tend to withdraw and become unresponsive. They don't want to deal with people; they want to focus on their work, so they retreat, keep their head down, and avoid interactions to keep things moving. If their work isn't acknowledged when stress is high, they begin to feel underappreciated and overlooked, thinking that their high level of contribution is being taken for granted. But you will rarely see a Reserved type outwardly fume or complain at work; they rarely publicize how they're really feeling. When they're not at their best, conversations become transactional—all work and no play.

Healthy-to-Stressed	
Actively lead the discussion, engage everyone, and seek input to arrive at the best solution	Withdraw from people and niceties to focus on getting the work done
Build strong relationships that support the work and help people feel seen and appreciated, personally and professionally	Indecisive and waits for others to lead and set the direction; avoid making decisions
Show more personality and infuse humor, keep things lighter	Push perspective to have influence; need to feel valued and appreciated
Use a combination of context and instinct to step into the conversation and make decisions	Feel angry (or hurt) that their contributions aren't being acknowledged and valued; hide their emotions and retreat
Genuinely connect with others on a personal level	Make conversations transactional; can be humorless, stiff, and quite serious

SECONDARY STYLE INFLUENCES

Secondary—Expressive

The Expressive style strengthens the quality and depth of a Reserved's working relationships. They become more outgoing and willing to connect with people on a personal level. An Expressive's easygoing and lighthearted nature nicely complements their more serious side, striking a good balance that allows interactions to be both productive and enjoyable. They become even easier to work with and more likable. Their ability to communicate effectively improves with an Expressive's verbal fluency and ability to read the room. Their capacity to lead collaborative teams and have influence also expands, and they're more inclined to address conflict when needed.

Secondary—Direct

The Reserved style gains more assertiveness and focus when paired with the Direct style. Their ability to keep conversations directed toward work is remarkable. They become adept at keeping people on task, providing thoughtful input, and sharing ideas that strengthen the team. They come prepared to advance the discussion and keep it focused.

They're clear and candid when they speak, keeping their emotions out of it. Interactions are primarily designed to be substantive and center around the outcomes needed to ensure the work is completed on time; this motivates them. Direct amplifies their serious nature, so it's important to watch for coming on too strong. Their all-work-and-no-play approach can feel impersonal to other styles that need a more human touch.

Secondary—Harmonious

When the Reserved style is paired with Harmonious, professional relationships often bridge into personal friendships. A Reserved individual often gains caring and supportive qualities that soften their more private nature, which strengthens the team dynamic; they patiently listen and learn from the experiences of others. They have the ability to foster deep connections that keep things running smoothly. Given that neither style likes to take the lead or step into conflict, they're more likely to sit back when decisions need to be made and when tensions build. They're much more comfortable waiting for someone to provide direction and carve out a role for them. This combination makes it more challenging when it comes to times when they need to be assertive or manage conflict.

Reserved at a Glance

Communication Needs	Maintain healthy working relationships
	Need to know that their input is valued
	Keep discussions on a professional level
	Share the big picture and the details
Value	Maintaining professional relationships, having influence, and contributing in a meaningful way that's valued by the team
Motivation	Ability to persuade and have influence
	Building professional relationships
	Being well-liked
Pace	Deliberate—steady, flexes to situational needs
Decision-Making	Influence—they like to weigh in and help determine the outcome, but they don't want the responsibility for making the final decision
Building Relationships	Focus on working together productively
	Friendly, stable, and nonconfrontational
	Provide constructive feedback to help people
Managing Conflict	Prefer to let others address conflict but will step in when needed

DIRECT

Responsible · Focused · Thorough · Candid · Independent

People who are Direct value communication that's substantive, brief, and produces results. This style represents the 22% of the population, and they're often responsible for keeping people on task. They're built for achievement and love to get right down to business in all forms of communication. They come prepared and work well in real time. They like to dive right into the subject matter, at a pace that advances the conversation at a solid clip.

They're energized by conversations that are purposeful and enjoy expressing their perspective and sharing ideas. For them, communication occupies the space between delivering information of value and asking clarifying questions that keep things moving. They appreciate discussions that are meaningful, but conversations that have no practical value or are unrelated to the work don't hold their interest. It takes everything they have to be patient when the conversation wanders into personal territory. They see tangents and small talk as a waste of time and bring the conversation back around to the task at hand as quickly as possible. They believe personal discussions belong outside of work.

They like to take the lead and enjoy the responsibility. Independent by nature, they're happy to make decisions on their own. They would much rather present a recommendation to the team than come to a decision by committee. Providing direction to others comes easily and they help to keep everyone focused on the outcomes needed. Ensuring that quality work is delivered on time motivates them. It feeds their need for achievement and provides a sense of control that puts them at ease.

While they appreciate what a team can produce together, they prefer to work on their own with more limited collaboration. Delivering work that's accurate is important to them and working alone gives them the time they need to concentrate and allows them to move at their own pace. Few understand how they accomplish all that they do. People who are Direct tend to be dependable, and it's one of the ways they build trust.

They're admired for their capability and knowledge and enjoy analyzing and sharing information. Providing insights and useful ideas that support the team is one way they foster connections. Having the respect of their coworkers is far more important to them than being well-liked. When they believe in something, they will argue their point. They don't shy away from disagreements or water down their opinions. Their straightforward, tell-it-like-it-is approach telegraphs sincerity, and when the pressure is on it can also be laced with impatience and judgment. They're not ones to equivocate and others appreciate knowing where they stand on issues. However, when they lock into a position and stop listening it can be off-putting to the other styles that prefer to have input and work toward agreements together.

Their directness is the quality that sets their style apart. When tensions arise, they will step into conflict when needed and tend to keep their emotions in check as they work toward resolution. They always have an opinion but give little away through their body language. These qualities add to their authoritative presence and prompt others to listen.

When they're fully present in conversations, they listen with an attentiveness that makes others feel heard and valued. They ask pointed questions to bring issues to the surface and gain additional insights, in search of deeper understanding and better solutions. But when a meeting or conversation drags on, they're apt to bring it to a close or make an excuse and leave.

Strengths	Weaknesses
• Clear, candid, straight to the point	• Blunt, abrasive, argumentative
• Results- and achievement-oriented	• Dominant, cold
• Keeps conversations on task and on time	• Impersonal, serious, strict
• Provides useful information and ideas	• Pushy, closed-minded, doesn't listen
• Decisive, self-assured	• Poor collaborator

STYLE EXPRESSIONS

The *healthy* expression of a Direct style brings out the best within them and others. They're more flexible in their approach and take the time to build connections with people. They share their thought processes and how they arrived at their recommendations. They inspire higher levels of accountability that produce quality work and better results. They balance their assertiveness with empathy to build consensus and resolve disagreements that keep the work flowing and the trains running on time.

But when they're carrying a heavy workload and feeling *stressed*, they accelerate and bulldoze over people to clear the fastest path to productivity. They become irritated when the conversation gets off track or veers into personal territory. They lose their finesse, overpower people, and push decisions through at a pace that eases their stress but creates more for everyone else.

Healthy-to-Stressed	
Inspire higher levels of personal responsibility within their team	Intolerant of the communication needs of others; can be a bit sharp in tone and manner and move too quickly
Intentional in their delivery, choose their words carefully; they're genuine, caring, and sincere	Tell others what to do and how to do it, don't listen, shoot down new ideas
Take time to listen and connect with people so they feel heard and valued	Allow frustration to get the best of them; steamroll over people and damage working relationships
Share information and ideas, discuss recommendations, and build alignment around decisions	Become overly candid and come off as cold or uncaring
Address issues with an openness and clarity that fosters trust and leads to resolution	Dominate the conversation, pick up the pace, and push forward

SECONDARY STYLE INFLUENCES

Secondary—Expressive

When Expressive is the secondary style for someone who's Direct, they keep the conversation productive and interesting. They lead discussions with an openness and honesty that helps others understand things more clearly. They tend to have strong points of view that are well informed and carry both rational and emotional appeal. Their ability to lead is enhanced, since it comes naturally to both styles; they share ideas, provide recommendations, and make decisions. They become more skilled at addressing conflict in ways that protect their relationships. The strength of this combination can feel overpowering to other styles that aren't as forthright or assertive. Creating space for other perspectives will make it easier for different styles to bring their voices into the conversation and add the value that comes from hearing diverse points of view.

Secondary—Reserved

The Reserved style amplifies the Direct's ability to focus, stay on task, and produce high-quality work. They're confident in their abilities and build professional relationships based on the quality of the work they produce. Maintaining their privacy is important; they have little tolerance for personal conversations and view small talk as a huge waste of time. They don't enjoy conversations that veer off course and will work to guide them back as quickly as possible, without damaging the relationship. There are also several complementary qualities that the Reserved style brings to someone who's Direct: They're easygoing and pleasant to work with, they're strong team players, and they care about helping people perform at their best. These traits soften them a bit and make them more approachable to other styles.

Secondary—Harmonious

While this is a rare style combination, the Direct person gains the connective qualities of the Harmonious style, which adds a warmth to the way they communicate and lead. They become more receptive to listening to the perspectives of others and considering different points of view. They're more gracious in their delivery—respectful and patient of the needs of others. They slow their pace and value bringing everyone along when the conversation is advancing to a decision point. They're also better able to keep their cool under pressure and look for ways to bring people together, which fosters a strong sense of team unity.

Direct at a Glance

Communication Needs	Keep conversations focused on work
	Make progress, stay on track, on time
	Get to the point and be brief
	Respect their input and knowledge
Value	Being responsible, staying on task, and delivering accurate work on time
Motivation	Results driven; accomplishment and productivity
	Respect for their capability and knowledge
	Precision that produces accurate work
Pace	Brisk—they speak at a quick clip and keep the conversation moving
Decision-Making	Independent—comfortable making decisions on their own and moving forward, even if others are not on board
Building Relationships	Sincere and honest, people know where they stand
	Consistently deliver accurate work on time
	Share information that helps others advance
Managing Conflict	Comfortable stepping into conflict

HARMONIOUS

Agreeable · Patient · Cooperative · Judicious · Caring

People with the Harmonious style are natural diplomats. They may represent the smallest group (16%), but they're often the glue that holds teams together and keeps the work flowing. They value creating supportive working relationships and protect them by keeping the peace. They steer clear of unnecessary conflict and try to avoid it when it does arise. While others have a need to shape the conversation with strong opinions, they take it all in and look for common ground. Theirs is the kind of mind that seeks to understand others and build bridges. Bringing people together and creating effective teams that get along well is incredibly motivating.

They enjoy being on healthy teams and are often the reason people work well together. If someone needs help on a project, they're always willing to lend a hand. They genuinely care about the people they work with and form lots of friendships that live outside the office. They instinctively know when people need encouragement and support, and coworkers are likely to seek them out when they need someone to listen, knowing their door is always open and that they'll offer their full attention. This makes them feel successful and valued.

They're not driven by a need to control people or situations, and don't force their opinions on others. They appreciate that healthy debate can be productive, but they prefer to listen and learn from the sidelines. They pay close attention to language and tone and are intolerant when people become disrespectful. They find it offensive when people flex their power or come on too strong in order to have their views prevail. They see it as unnecessary and destructive.

They spend more time listening than any other style. They're happy to let the conversation run its course, asking an occasional question. They value hearing different perspectives and considering their merit. They like to have time to process information, organize their thoughts, and form their opinions before they speak up. Once they've heard the different viewpoints, they share their views in a way that acknowledges what others have said. If the tension is high or there are too many strong voices in the room, they may need to be invited into the conversation, but when they do share their opinion, it's grounded in insights that help others to see a fuller picture. They're known for bringing a people-focused perspective that other styles often overlook when making decisions. They care deeply that the human impact be thoughtfully considered.

When they're put on the spot or asked to share their opinion in the moment, it can be difficult to immediately put their thoughts into words. In these situations, they wade in and favor a "float it out there" approach. They don't want to offend anyone, so their language is more tentative and exploratory. They don't push, and they don't like to *be* pushed. If they're feeling pressured, they may even say what they believe their fellow team members or boss want to hear and comply with the group to find a path out. Some mistakenly confuse the Harmonious style's desire to keep things peaceful with a lack of caring, when it's really that they value their relationships far more than having their views prevail.

When it comes to making decisions, they prefer to provide input and then defer to those in authority. While they want to be heard, they don't enjoy taking on the responsibility for making the ultimate call. However, when a Harmonious style is leading the team and must make a decision, they consult those who will be affected by their choices to ensure they take their needs into consideration. They look at all sides of the situation, deliberate, and then decide. Their inclusive design often leads to successful outcomes, but it can frustrate Direct types who prefer a faster pace and a more independent approach.

When there are gaps in a discussion, they'll wait for others to jump in and fill the void. They have no need to dominate. While skilled at small talk, they like it when someone else carries the conversation. They're deliberate and prepared when they take the lead. There's a thoughtfulness that permeates the way they deliver information that makes people receptive to their ideas. Their facial expressions are open, their tone even, and their pace keeps everyone engaged. Words are chosen with care, in order to put people at ease and avoid any unnecessary conflict. They work to prevent misunderstandings whenever possible and often use humor to lighten the mood when tensions arise.

Strengths	Weaknesses
Diplomatic, gracious	Passive, too deferential
Good listeners, caring	Too quiet, don't speak up
Supportive, relationship-focused	Enabling, too tolerant
Judicious, thoughtful	Overly cautious, risk-averse
Cooperative, keep their cool	Avoid conflict, hold in their emotions

STYLE EXPRESSIONS

When the Harmonious style is in its *healthy* expression, they confidently use their voice to share their insights and shape the discussion. They bring a "human" perspective to decision-making and raise the level of thinking. They're able to address tensions that are destructive to the team so people can resolve their differences and work together productively.

If they're feeling *stressed*, they're prone to limiting their interactions with colleagues and treading lightly. When strong personalities or conflict overwhelms them, they will quickly defer and agree to whatever is needed to avoid damaging their relationships. They become quiet and withdrawn, hoping to stay off the battleground. They're overly compliant and bury any frustration they feel to keep the peace.

Healthy-to-Stressed	
Genuine when sharing their perspective and have a clear point of view	Water down opinions, restate what has been said, or say nothing at all
Contribute at a high level and offer up potential solutions	Become exceptionally quiet, waiting to be asked to share their thoughts
Stay engaged when tensions arise, proactively working to resolve conflict	Avoid conflict and discussing issues that may create tension
Confidently make decisions and factor in the human side of things	Enable others to take the lead; avoid making a decision
Support their colleagues when they're able to do so and set healthy boundaries	Hold in emotions and become overly compliant and cooperative

SECONDARY STYLE INFLUENCES

Secondary—Expressive

The Harmonious and Expressive styles share more characteristics than any other combination. Both styles are people-oriented, which strengthens their ability to make a personal connection and bring the energy that uplifts others. They use humor well to keep things light. Skilled at reading the room, they're able to see what people need and how to best support them. They're also good at reading people's intentions and can spot a hidden agenda a mile away.

The Expressive qualities nicely complement Harmonious by layering in the strength of assertiveness and confidence that enhances their ability to lead.

They're able to pick up their pace and respond more quickly. They step into the conversation, share their opinions more readily, and are more comfortable addressing conflict. They're also better at proactively problem-solving.

Secondary—Reserved

The Reserved style strengthens a Harmonious person's natural ability to connect with people. They build strong, lasting relationships that often turn into deep friendships that extend outside of work. They love to be part of a team and like to contribute in a meaningful way. They also bring a stability to the team that allows it to run smoothly and be more successful. Given that neither style likes to take the lead or step into conflict, they're more likely to sit back when decisions need to be made and tensions build. They're more comfortable waiting for someone to provide direction than to step into that role.

Secondary—Direct

This style combination may seem like a paradox, but it does occasionally happen. The Direct style strengthens the Harmonious person's ability to speak up when they disagree. They're incredibly deliberate and come prepared to express their point of view. They openly share ideas and information that will help others, and they ground their perspective with facts. These communicators are often known as the "practical ones." Being productive and keeping the work flowing motivates them; they want to contribute at a high level and see their team succeed. They build trusted working relationships by being honest and dependable.

Harmonious at a Glance

Communication Needs	Safe and respectful environment
	Time to process and form opinions
	Friendly and smooth interactions
	Others to take the lead, provide direction
Value	Working on peaceful teams; protecting their work relationships; listening to and supporting others
Motivation	Keeping the peace
	Feeling safe and secure
	Ensuring people are treated respectfully
Pace	Slower, more cautious
Decision-Making	Consultative—thoughtfully weigh in and are happy to defer to others; seek input from all affected when they must make the call
Building Relationships	Warm, friendly, agreeable
	Supportive of others and their needs
	Respectful, patient, and a good listener
Managing Conflict	Avoids conflict

CHAPTER 7

Mastering Your Communication Style

*T*he most important relationship you'll ever have is with yourself. This means understanding who you are, what drives the way you interact with people, and how you can proactively maintain your well-being. Your relationship with yourself sets the tone for how you think, feel, act, communicate, and listen and, like all great relationships, you have to invest in it. Cultivating positive change requires that you learn to accurately see yourself fully—your talents, your motivations, your imperfections, and how you impact others. Only then can you learn to manage your thoughts and behaviors. If there's only one thing you take away from this book let it be this: develop a deeper understanding of yourself so you can build positive, trusted working relationships and find more purpose in what you do.

Ultimately, mastering your communication style is about learning how to express yourself from the healthiest position you can in every situation. This means you're able to stay consciously connected to your thoughts and emotions, proactively manage your well-being, and use your enhanced self-awareness to be intentional about what you say and do.

Our level of conscious awareness and well-being are constantly in flux, so it takes practice and self-reflection to communicate from this level. Remember: Our goal isn't to communicate from a perfectly healthy expression 100% of the time. That would be impossible. Life is filled with ups and downs and we're bound to make mistakes from time to time. But the goal is to continually elevate how we communicate when we're on autopilot, until we're at our best more often than not. Communicating from health 70% to 90% of the time is achievable. *But* it takes concerted practice. Mastering your communication style doesn't happen overnight; your skills will expand and evolve as you expand and evolve.

SELF-AWARENESS IS ALWAYS THE FIRST STEP

It's impossible to improve your communication skills if you aren't able to see where you need to grow. In order to even touch mastery, you need to develop a high level of self-awareness to gain insights into how you communicate. Understanding your communication style is a big first step in that direction—your style breakdown will help you to recognize your communication patterns, leverage your strengths, compensate for your weaknesses, and stay mindful of what drives you. Just as important, you'll get better at seeing what each style needs and how those differing needs can create tension.

Self-awareness is a foundational life skill that's central to your ability to build and elevate your communication skills. You need to be able to clearly and objectively see yourself and how you're contributing to a situation. You need to be able to recognize what's really motivating you. And you need to be able to accurately see how you impact others. When self-awareness is low, you're far more likely to take things personally, project, or blame others, which leads to more misunderstandings and more stress. It's not always easy to identify your limiting patterns and what they stir up. But through reflection you'll begin to better see yourself and understand what drives you, and once you become aware of a limiting behavior, it's hard to un-see. And that's a good thing! Because once you can see it, you can change it.

As difficult as it is to recognize our less-than-desirable qualities, it can also be equally challenging to see our strengths and the positive impact we have on people. (We're complicated!) We discount what comes easily and think anyone can do what we do just as well (or better), but they can't. Instead, we focus on our weaker qualities and beat ourselves up for having any flaws at all. Clearly this isn't helpful! And then there are the times we're completely blind to what we're doing, or in denial that we're the ones creating the problem.

Our capacity to accurately see and understand ourselves expands over the course of our lives. Increasing our level of self-awareness is a need that never seems to be satisfied—even (and perhaps especially) for those of us who think we have exceptional self-awareness. After all, studies have shown that most of us think we know ourselves quite well, and far better than we actually do. Remarkably, 95% of people questioned expressed that they were either somewhat or very self-aware; however, researchers have found that the number of people with strong self-awareness skills is actually closer to 12% to 15%; these stats hold up whether you're looking at someone's ability to evaluate their leadership skills or how well they perform at work or even how well they drive a car. We're just not that good at seeing ourselves if roughly 80% of us have a massive gap between our self-perceptions and our true understanding of who we are. If you're thinking, *Well, I'm sure I fall into the group that actually has high self-awareness*, know this: those with the *lowest* competency in self-awareness frequently hold the *highest* levels of confidence in their abilities.[1]

This probably isn't all that surprising when it comes to communication. We all work with people who grossly misjudge how effectively they express themselves. The boss who thinks she's exceptional at managing conflict and fails to see she's just strong-arming everyone into compliance. The tone-deaf client who dominates every conversation while reminding everyone of the importance of listening. A colleague who delivers brutal feedback and yet is convinced he's an inspiring mentor. Our gaps in awareness seem to be obvious to everyone but us.

The good news is that self-awareness is a skill we can all develop and when we do there are all kinds of benefits. Self-awareness not only improves our communication skills but also helps us build stronger relationships and make better decisions. It improves our ability to see how we affect others, expands our empathy, and helps us stay open to new perspectives. It also leads to higher levels of job satisfaction and happiness. And perhaps most important, self-awareness is linked to lowering levels of anxiety, stress, and depression, which all affect our well-being.

Expanding our self-awareness creates a virtuous cycle that elevates our ability to communicate from health, which allows us to build trust, improve our relationships, and strengthen our well-being again and again. Clearly, self-awareness is a worthy pursuit!

Self-awareness is often described like an onion: you peel back layer after layer as you access a new levels of understanding. I prefer to think of self-awareness as a rose—one that gradually opens as we step more fully into seeing and being ourselves; as we expand our awareness new petals reveal more of the depth and beauty that we've always possessed. It's a journey toward self-revelation and the unfurling of Self that happens over time as we pay closer attention to our thoughts, emotions, and patterns of communication. Self-exploration isn't a code we crack, or a life hack, that once conquered exposes everything you need to know about yourself all at once. It's a progression. We gain degrees of self-understanding over time, as we take in new insights about ourselves. Bit by bit and day by day we learn to see who we are and who we're capable of being.

The first step on the path to expanding self-awareness is to become well acquainted with your communication style. Go back to the communication style profiles in the previous chapter; reflect on them and start noticing how and when the behaviors of your primary and secondary styles show up at work. Every moment of self-recognition, every spark of "Oh yeah, that's me," gives you a great start on your journey. The exercises and practices ahead will also help you to become more aware of how you communicate and where you can continue to grow. You'll become very familiar with your style in health and under stress and begin to recognize where there are gaps to close. You'll learn how to play to your strengths and manage your weaknesses. And you'll discover how much faster self-awareness comes when you pause to reflect on and learn from your experiences.

EXERCISES FOR UNDERSTANDING YOUR COMMUNICATION STYLE

While personal insights come in a flash, change comes over time through practice. Some of the exercises in this section are intended to spark those "aha" moments, while others are here to help you convert those breakthroughs in self-awareness into deeper connections; the kind that inspire you to grow and help you see where things need to evolve.

Say you have one of those "aha" moments when you suddenly see a connection between your energy level and how confident you feel sharing your opinions in a team meeting; you realize that when you're feeling good you share your ideas with an enthusiasm that's contagious and people start building on them. And so you make it a practice to boost your energy before a meeting so that you have more positive energy that helps everything run more smoothly. Perhaps you see how you dominate conversations when you're under pressure and recognize that you're the reason others may be afraid to speak up. Or maybe you suddenly realize that being too agreeable ultimately damages the relationship you were trying to protect, and that what colleagues need from you is critical thinking that expands the potential of an idea. Learning to stay tuned in to your emotions, stress level, and impact on others is key to building self-awareness and accessing new levels of growth.

As your self-awareness grows, you'll begin to observe how you connect with people at work in different situations. You'll become more attuned to what's needed in the moment and how to play to your strengths. Experience is life's greatest teacher, and a little reflection allows you to see what's working for you and what's not. And just like that your awareness begins to blossom.

Recognize the Gap Between Health and Stress

As our levels of awareness and well-being fluctuate we tend to move back and forth between the healthy and stressed expressions of our style—even in the course of just one day! Typically, we start out strong and slide into lower-level expressions of our style as the day wears on and our stress builds or when someone says something that sets us off. The good news is that we all have the ability to course correct if we stay mindful of what we say and do. Self-awareness is the key to communicating well. You need to know what it looks like for you when you're communicating in health and under stress. The more you understand yourself, the faster you'll see when your behavior is shifting into a danger zone. This level of awareness allows you to change your response so that you don't create interpersonal tensions that add more stress.

Given that we're all unique, it's important to identify, specifically, what your style looks like when you're in health and under stress. This reflection practice will also help you to see how the gap between your expressions shows up for you. Your goal is to identify the behaviors that signal you're moving from a healthy expression into a more troublesome stressed response.

These changes look different from person to person, and some are more obvious than others. Some styles have big swings in behavior that are easy to recognize and others are subtler and require you to pay close attention to your internal dialogue. For example, an Expressive under stress is more obvious when they suddenly become sarcastic or extremely quiet and withdrawn, whereas the behaviors of people with a Harmonious style don't look all that different even when they're extremely stressed. In fact, they may become even *more* agreeable as their cooperative nature shifts into compliance. Their signals happen internally, and when they stay mindful they'll see a significant difference in their thoughts, emotions, and motivations.

For this first exercise, I'd like you to reflect back on your primary and secondary styles to capture what it looks like when *you* communicate in health and under stress. Refer back to the style profiles beginning on page 67. As tempting as it might be to make your list on a computer, I strongly encourage you to write your reflections down on paper. The sheer act of writing slows down your mind and connects you to style insights on a deeper level. It forces your brain to mentally engage with the ideas in a way that encodes them into your memory and strengthens recall. Perhaps most important, handwriting sharpens your critical thinking and ability to connect the dots, since you process the information as you're recording it.[2] This practice helps you to see new insights, and since you're looking to strengthen your self-awareness, why not give yourself every advantage you can?

EXERCISE: What Are My Tells?

To begin, take a piece of paper and draw a line down the center to create two columns. Label one "Healthy" and the other "Stressed." Go back through your style profiles and write down five behaviors or key phrases that reflect the way you show up most often when you're at your best in the "Healthy" column, then do the same looking at how you communicate at your worst and write those key words in the "Stressed" column.

Once you've captured what resonates from your style profile(s), use the questions below to help you dig a little deeper into the influences that shape what you say and do. To help you get specific, picture a situation where you were communicating from health, then from stress, as you reflect on the following questions:

- How do you see yourself in the moment? What does that moment of healthy/stressed communication feel like in your body?
- What thoughts are running through your mind? What are you saying to yourself?
- What flags go up to tell you how you're expressing yourself? Are there thoughts, emotions, or behaviors that tell you where you're at?
- Identify the key influences that drive the way you engage. Do you have certain beliefs or values that determine how you behave? Are there certain people or situations that impact you more than others? What role does stress and well-being play?
- What are you thinking and feeling once the conversation is over?

How Do You Impact Others?

How we communicate has the power to create a ripple within teams and organizations, much the same way that dropping a pebble into a still pond sends an expanding series of ripples in all directions. Sometimes we're able to see our impact, sometimes we aren't. And then there are the times we completely misread how we're affecting people.

If you really want to understand how you impact others, you need to look at yourself from two perspectives: internal (inside out) and external (outside in). Think of internal self-awareness as the insights that only you can see because they require full knowledge of what you think and feel. You are the only one with full access to your beliefs, values, thoughts, intentions, emotions, and perspectives, which is why some insights can only come through reflection and introspection. Cultivating your capacity to clearly see how you affect others is critical to your ability to elevate your communication skills.

There are other insights that can only be gained through an outside point of view; they show you the blind spots between how you see yourself and how others experience you. This is why developing your external self-awareness is equally important—it allows you to see yourself through someone else's eyes. Only by seeing ourselves from an outside perspective do we get the full picture of how we're impacting our colleagues.

It's not easy to accurately see how we affect people, both for better and worse. I've had clients who underestimate the positive impact they have on their teams even when they've been told; they just don't hear it or appreciate how meaningful it is. Conversely, I've worked with others who fail to see the negative influence they have on people. They rationalize their behavior and minimalize the fallout. Remember, it's unlikely that anyone will tell you directly when you're doing something that they hate or damaging the relationship, especially if you're in a position of authority. You'll have to ask.

It takes courage to seek feedback. On some level we all fear what we might hear. No one enjoys hearing that they've caused someone to feel pain, discomfort, or diminished. It hurts to realize how your poor behavior has affected others. But you can't change what you're unaware of.

Sometimes people worry that asking for feedback will make them look weak. They couldn't be more wrong. In fact, studies have shown that people's estimation of you *rises* when you seek feedback: 83% of top-performing leaders proactively solicit feedback on a regular basis,[3] and these leaders are also viewed as more effective by their employees, peers, and bosses. Soliciting feedback demonstrates to their teams that they want to be and do better, which inspires people to want to work with them—and for them.

<hr />

EXERCISE: Seek Feedback

For this exercise you'll need to ask at least three people who know you well— and who you trust will be honest with you—to share how you come across when you're communicating day to day. Their feedback will help you identify where you're landing on the healthy-to-stressed continuum of the different aspects of your style. It's important to get input from a variety of people who can reflect different angles and perspectives: mentors, managers, clients, vendors, peers, and those who play supporting roles. You may find that, even when asked, people are hesitant to offer feedback and give constructive input. Be sure to let them know how much you value their opinions, and encourage them to be honest. And give them some time to consider their feedback so that they can be thoughtful—a week or two is usually enough.

The simplest approach is to give each person the following three questions and be sure to request that they provide you with a couple of specific examples to help illustrate what they're seeing. The more specific the feedback the more valuable it will be:

- When I'm communicating well, what impact do I have on you, my team, my clients, etc.?
- When I'm *not* communicating well, what impact do I have on you, my team, my clients, etc.?
- What's one area where I seem to be blind to the impact I'm having on you, my team, my clients, etc.?

Once you have all your responses, look for the patterns and themes that emerge from the different perspectives. What do they have in common? Are there situational aspects that impact the way you communicate? Make sure to fully appreciate *all* of the ways you're effective in how you engage (it's easy to focus on the negative, so soak in the positive feedback too!).

Sometimes the feedback you receive makes it easy to see where you can improve. If that's the case, focus on shifting your approach in that area. If your feedback is more general or you're uncertain where to begin, select a behavior from the healthy expression of your style that you'd like to strengthen—one that you feel will improve your interactions the most. Another idea is to start by working to develop your listening skills; becoming a better listener always improves communication. Or you may know that you have a behavior that shows up under stress that you'd like to better manage, in which case you can develop strategies to help you manage your way through those situations.

There are any number of ways to become an elevated communicator. Select one area where you know you can improve how you engage with people and get started. Experiment and see what approaches work best for you. Once you feel you've got these new behaviors in place, select another and keep building.

Genuine self-awareness is a rare quality. People who have cultivated it appreciate the insights that an outside perspective provides—it's how they're able to see their biases and blind spots. When you make it a practice to seek external input twice a year, you'll find you become more and more aware of who you are and how you impact the world around you. It's a valuable tool for elevating your communication skills and leveling up the trust between you and your colleagues. And it only works if you use it.

LEVERAGING STRENGTHS AND MINIMIZING WEAKNESSES

As you become more aware of your communication style, it's likely that you're already seeing how your strengths have supported the achievements you've had in your career or moments when you've felt most fulfilled in your role. For example, an Expressive might recall a moment when their ability to put people at ease helped them land a new client. Or a Direct might take pride in how their clarity and precision help them cut through to what matters and provide valuable direction for their team.

Seeing the connection between your communication strengths and your successes builds more confidence and inspires you to keep developing and leveraging your skills. You feel more secure and use your voice more powerfully. The ability to communicate effectively enhances all of your talents and skills. This is why it's so important to learn to dial up your communication strengths and leverage their benefits. You can also use your strengths to help you minimize your communication weaknesses.

Your style's weaknesses are where you're more likely to create and experience challenges in your work. Some are tied to our personalities or lack of awareness (like being too assertive and coming across as intimidating or dominant), but others are communication skills that are underdeveloped (like listening or addressing conflict). Your style weaknesses can also be strengths that have been misused or taken to an extreme and become your Achilles' heel. For example, Reserved people are exceptionally strong team players but there are times when they also need to feel like the team captain. If their need to have more influence than others gets the best of them for too long, it can destroy the team spirit.

EXERCISE: Do This, Not That

Learning to play to your strengths and minimize your weaknesses is much easier when you're crystal clear about what your behavior looks like. Take a sheet of paper, or use your journal, and draw a line down the middle of the page to create two columns. Label one "Do More of This" and the other "Stop Doing This."

Now read through the strengths and healthy expressions of your primary and secondary communication styles. Decide what feels accurate for you. Make a list of the specific behaviors that make you an effective communicator under the "Do More of This" column. Do the same for your weaknesses and stressed expressions for both of your styles, this time recording behaviors and habits that come to mind in the "Stop Doing This" column. Remember, be specific about the behaviors you want to stop doing; the more clearly you capture the behaviors you'd like to change, the faster you'll see them.

Once you have both columns filled in, take a step back and compare them, looking for ways you can use your strengths to minimize or neutralize your weaknesses. For example, say an Expressive recognizes they easily intimidate people and notes "Don't come on too strong" under their "Stop Doing This" column. To help minimize this behavior, they could lean on their ability to "put people at ease" and add that direction to their "Do More of This" column.

Each week choose one strength to optimize and one weakness to minimize. Keep this list handy until it becomes second nature to offer up your talents and manage around your weaknesses. The more visible it is, the easier it will be to practice putting your ideas into action.

The bottom line on strengths and weaknesses is this: The more intentionally you communicate, the more effective you'll be. Leveraging your strengths and minimizing your weaknesses makes it easier to build trust, be productive, and feel more satisfaction at work. And, in case it's not obvious, as your communication skills grow you experience less stress and more well-being.

Pause and Reflect

Most of us are so busy trying to keep up at work that we don't fully appreciate how slowing down allows us to go faster. Creating time to pause, reflect, and learn from our experiences makes it easier to communicate mindfully, with intention, and sets the stage for us to access the healthiest expression of our style.

People who are willing to pause and reflect for just 15 minutes at the end of each day have been shown to outperform their coworkers by 23%. Research has also shown that people who use their commuting time to plan their day and reflect on it experienced more productivity, more happiness, and less burnout.[4]

Self-reflection is a powerful tool for raising your awareness around how your communication style impacts your working relationships, productivity, and well-being. It allows you to make connections between your inner state of well-being and how you're expressing yourself. It helps you to process your thoughts, perceptions, emotions, and attitudes. It offers an opportunity to question what you're thinking and feeling, to see if you're pulling up an old story or mindset that's making work more difficult than it needs to be. It gives you a chance to become curious about what drives you and how you operate. And it empowers you to take personal responsibility for how you communicate.

EXERCISE: Pause and Reflect

Putting your thoughts down on paper helps you to see your communication patterns more clearly. Carve out 15 minutes at the end of the day to learn from your experiences. Set a timer and, in a journal or on a piece of paper, write down any moments, experiences, feelings, or thoughts that felt particularly salient over the course of your day. Pay particular attention to your emotions and behaviors. Remember, if you look at the thoughts that created your feelings and drove your behaviors, you'll gain some rich insights into what lies beneath the surface. If you're feeling stuck, below are a few thought prompts to help you get started.

- **Any big style swings?** Take a look at what expression of your communication style was leading today. Were you mostly on autopilot or did you swing around? You may find that some days you run the whole gamut from healthy to stressed. If that's the case, take a closer look to see what's causing you to shift. Were you triggered? Stressed out? Were you around coworkers whose styles complement or conflict with yours?

- **What were the highlights?** See if you can pinpoint what contributed to your standout moments so you can repeat them tomorrow. Were you actively listening? Were you paying attention to how you were impacting others?

- **What am I dwelling on**? Are there any conversations you keep replaying in your mind? A story you'll share later when someone asks about your day? The stories we tell others often hold a great deal of information that can be mined to strengthen our self-awareness. What is it about the situation that still has you thinking about it? Take a look at your behavior to more clearly see the role you played. How did you come across? What did you say or decide not to say? What were you thinking and feeling in the moment? Try looking at the situation from everyone's perspective. Examine your behavior and see what you can learn about yourself.

- **What did I avoid?** Were there any conversations you steered clear of today? If so, take a closer look at what's underneath your reluctance to step into those conversations. How long have you been putting them off? How often do you think about these unresolved issues? What would make you feel safe enough to address what you're avoiding?

- **Any trust issues?** Do any of your working relationships feel like they're shifting? If so, look at what's driving the change in the relationship. Has the trust level dipped? Was there some event that set things in motion?

- **Any do-overs?** What conversations did you find challenging? What role did you play in creating the challenge? How could it have gone better? What would you do differently?

We work in fast-paced, results-oriented, and often frenetic business environments, where the days blend together and weeks fly by. And yet our ability to communicate and lead requires that we make time and space to reflect and learn. When we make it a priority to pause and reflect, we grow.

As important as it is to notice all the dynamics that influence how well we communicate, it's not enough to just notice. We need to be able to do something with the insights we gain about ourselves. A big part of getting to know yourself and seeing how stress affects you is so that you can recognize when it's time to take care of yourself.

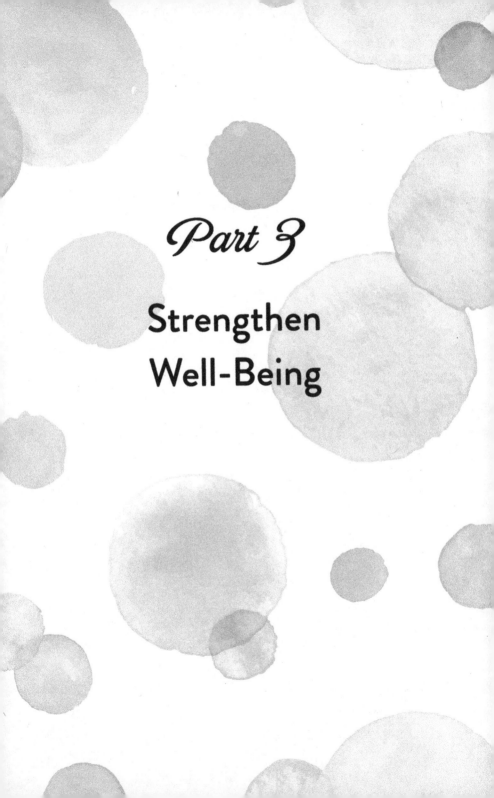

Part 3

Strengthen Well-Being

CHAPTER 8

Renew Your Energy

*I*t's no secret that workplace stress is having a massive impact on our physical, emotional, and mental health. Even so, we don't always recognize how it impacts our ability to communicate in healthy ways. We tend to think of stress as a consequence of our jobs, but interpersonal issues frequently create more stress than the job itself.

When our well-being is low, we experience a disconnect between our self-awareness and how we express ourselves, which only leads to more misunderstandings and difficulties in our working relationships. Our interactions are more likely to stir up insecurities, frustrations, and resentment which adds to our stress and erodes trust. This means that how we communicate plays a vital role in maintaining or disrupting personal well-being *and* that our well-being directly impacts how effectively we communicate.

If we want to take full advantage of our communication strengths, we have to elevate our baseline wellness. Put another way, our goal is to set ourselves up for success by building the strongest possible foundation for communicating from the healthy expression of our styles. To do that we have to take a hard look at our physical, emotional, and mental wellness. You may not realize it but deficits in rest, positivity, and even friendships can have an adverse impact on our foundations. By tending to our well-being we're able to keep shifting our autopi-lot responses closer and closer to the healthy expressions of our style.

WHY WE PUSH THROUGH AND BURN OUT

Our sense of self-worth has become so wrapped up in our obsession with pro-ductivity and accomplishment that we routinely push through until we "hit the wall," even when we know better. Most of us respond to increasing work de-mands by putting in more hours, which inevitably makes us more stressed, less productive, and far less effective—both at the tasks we're trying to accomplish and in our communication with others.

It's easy to get caught up in an endless spin cycle that drains our energy until we're running on empty and, sadly, we often wait until we're in crisis before we make it a priority to take care of ourselves. These days we're so overworked, chronically stressed, and "always on" that we're burning out in record numbers. So much so that the World Health Organization has now classified burnout as a syndrome that results from "chronic workplace stress that has not been success-fully managed." Job burnout is specifically related to work stress—feelings of physical or emotional energy depletion or exhaustion that also involves negativ-ity and cynicism, reduced efficacy, and loss of personal identity.[1]

Studies show that a whopping 77% of employees have experienced burnout in their current job and 91% have unmanageable amounts of stress.[2] Yet as much as we'd like to think otherwise, finding a job that fills us with purpose—or even one we're passionate about—doesn't prevent us from feeling extreme stress. We subscribe to a cultural narrative that taking a break will put us so far behind that one-third of employees don't feel comfortable taking vacation time.[3] We barely pause for lunch at our desk.

We've been so conditioned to prioritize work over all else that we can't even see how shortsighted we're being. Even when our employers encourage us to take care of ourselves, we hesitate. For example, I've helped companies create well-being programs to reduce stress countless times, and while everyone says they wish they had more time to take care of themselves, when presented with the opportunity to do so they pass. I've shown teams loads of research that proves how taking periodic breaks actually helps you to refresh your focus and get more done,[4] but I've found that the biggest hurdle to getting people to use their company's on-site meditation room isn't convincing them that meditation is beneficial, it's convincing them to stop working for five minutes. They believe in the restorative powers of meditation; they just don't believe meditation is more beneficial than pushing through.

We've convinced ourselves that "powering through" and getting ahead is the path to safety and security. Many of us came up through the ranks under management styles that instilled fear and competition to improve people's performance. We were conditioned to believe that the more we worked the more valuable we were to our employers. This played right into our survival instincts. It's no wonder that we struggle to pause and give ourselves a moment to breathe, and why we value sending one more email over our own well-being. It's not easy when our survival instincts compete for our time and attention. We can choose to prioritize our emotional selves (self-worth) or our physical selves (renewal). A complicated bind!

The Symptoms of Burnout

While "burnout" isn't a medical diagnosis, many experts think that other conditions—like anxiety and depression—are behind it. For some, their job may not be the main cause, but they're more likely to recognize the symptoms of burnout faster at work. No matter what the main cause, job burnout can affect your physical and mental health.

If you find that you're experiencing burnout, anxiety, or depression, *please seek professional help*. It's important to take care of your health and well-being on all levels!

The Mayo Clinic lists burnout symptoms that we all need to be aware of:[5]

- becoming cynical or critical at work
- dragging yourself to work and having trouble getting started

- becoming irritable or impatient with coworkers, customers, or clients
- lacking the energy to be consistently productive
- difficulty concentrating
- lack of satisfaction from your achievements
- feeling disillusioned about your job
- using food, drugs, or alcohol to feel better (or to not feel)
- change in sleep patterns
- bothered by unexplained headaches, stomach or bowel problems, or other physical complaints

The fact of the matter is that none of us can sustain peak performance forever. So, we can either make it a priority to invest in our energy and empower ourselves, or we can ignore the signals that tell us we need to recharge and continue to struggle. We've all experienced how much easier it is to lead a meeting, make decisions, or have a difficult conversation when we're feeling energized. We've also experienced how quickly we can become short-tempered and easily distracted when we're depleted. How we experience life is largely up to us and whether we take care of ourselves. The truth is that we have more control over our well-being than we realize or utilize.

TRAPPED IN THE STRESS SPIRAL

We live and work in cultures that have conditioned us to believe that speed is power, slowing down shows weakness, and that weakness is unacceptable. Common sense will tell you that too much stress without adequate recovery negatively affects well-being and compounds communication challenges. But most of us are looking for an escape and hoping it serves as a recovery. For many this means hitting the couch and grabbing the remote as soon as possible. We binge on whatever Netflix or Hulu is serving up, while simultaneously scrolling through our social media and newsfeeds. Others eat their stress or drink their cares away. No matter how it shows up, we crave that "me time" when we're off the clock and don't have to answer to anyone. The problem is that "me time" typically starts around 9:00 p.m., and if you have kids, it might be hours before no one is demanding your attention, the house is quiet, and you can finally just collapse on the couch and relax.

The more concerning problem is that few of our most common relaxation activities actually renew our energy or restore well-being. In fact, most of our stress-relief behaviors keep us in a perpetual cycle of depletion. We scroll through social media to feel more connected, only to end up feeling more isolated, anxious, and depressed. We stay up too late and sleep too little, which makes the next day even harder. Have you ever noticed how much you crave sugar and caffeine when you haven't had a good night's sleep? That's because your body is looking for the fuel it's lacking. And we end up making expedient choices that spike our energy until we crash, and round and round we go.

EXERCISE: Limit Your Scrolling

If you want to increase feelings of well-being, create a healthy relationship with social media. Set some boundaries in the form of time limits. You can even activate some settings within the apps to manage your off and on times, like Twitter's sleep settings, so it requires no thought. If you notice that you're beginning to feel any emotion other than joy (such as jealousy, insecurity, or FOMO), take a break from all screens and go do something you enjoy. Or—if you're late-night scrolling—just go to bed and catch up on your sleep.

Our bodies need *at least* seven hours of rest a night, but more than a third of American adults aren't getting the sleep they need on a regular basis. Without sleep, we increase our risk of developing chronic conditions like obesity, diabetes, high blood pressure, and heart disease, as well as strong and frequent mental distress.[6] In the moment staying up late feels good, but the next day you can't think straight or manage your emotions.

YES, YOU HAVE TO SLEEP!

If you've ever experienced a disrupted night's sleep, you already know how much harder it is to gather your thoughts, pay attention, and listen when you're exhausted. And while it might seem obvious, it's essential to understand just how integral our physical energy is to our ability to communicate. Too often we're willing to trade sleep for completing more tasks or watching just one more show on Netflix in the name of relaxation—failing to see that we're digging a deeper hole for ourselves to climb out of.

Effective communication relies on a well-rested and well-functioning mind and body. There's a direct correlation between our physical energy and our cognitive abilities, and when our reasoning, memory, problem solving, or decision-making are impaired our capacity for effective communication decreases sharply.[7] Fatigue also negatively impacts our ability to empathize and process emotion well, and its effect on our mood is pronounced.[8] It's no wonder we're more irritable and argumentative when we're tired!

On some level we know that it's impossible for the brain and body to function properly when we push through, don't get enough rest, or take a break, and yet we all do it from time to time. Research has repeatedly shown that when we're sleep-deprived for even one night we become far more emotionally reactive. Brain imaging studies have shown that the amygdala (the deep emotional brain center) becomes overly responsive by 60% when we don't get adequate sleep; its hypersensitivity primes us to be emotionally triggered into fight, flight, or freeze responses. We lose our ability to manage our behavior and become reactive, which makes us more volatile in stressful situations.[9]

We've all experienced when our emotions spill over and it's rarely pretty. When we're exhausted, we easily slip into the stress side of our communication style. What would normally be a small annoyance becomes intolerable. People start to get on your nerves and, if you're not careful, you end up saying or doing something that makes matters worse. It's that moment when your quick wit turns to sarcasm to let everyone know how you really feel. Or maybe you're the type who withdraws from conversations that frustrate you, leaving it to the most dominant voices to hash out an imperfect solution. We all have our ways of coping when we're just too tired to care anymore. Rarely do those coping mechanisms serve us.

When well-being is high . . .	When well-being is low . . .
Respond with intention	Emotionally reactive
Open-minded	Critical
Listen	Shut down
Express empathy	Project or personalize
Stay curious	Become judgmental
Seek support	Avoid people
Understanding, fair	Dominate, attack, or withdraw
Patient, tolerant	Impatient, interruptive, pushy

SMALL CHANGES
CAN CHANGE EVERYTHING

Most of us don't stop to think about how much energy we have or need, we just get up when we can't hit the snooze button any longer and make our way through the day (day after day after day). When you live out of balance for so long, feeling depleted begins to seem normal. It's hard to even remember what it feels like to be rested, let alone energized. It can even feel hard to find the energy to change your habits and create wellness routines that you *want to make*. But if you start small and build, those small steps will add up over time and set you on your way. And for most people, making a small change is more approachable and sustainable.

The simplest, most impactful place to start is by making sleep a priority. Most of us know that, on average, we need seven to nine hours of sleep to perform well. But did you know that it's even more important to wake up at the same time every morning? A consistent wake-up time will actually help you sleep better at night. It also sharpens your focus, brightens your mood, strengthens your immune system, and improves your job performcance. Even better, you can feel the benefits within a week or two. It doesn't take long for your body to appreciate a consistent rhythm.[10]

EXERCISE: Power Up with a Nap!

A power nap is an easy way to renew your energy and boost productivity. Taking a short, 15- to 20-minute nap in the early afternoon helps to regulate emotions, lower stress, strengthen your immune system, and improve performance![11] After 20 minutes, do a few yoga stretches, go for a quick walk, or get some sunlight to signal to your body that your nap is over and it's time to focus again.

If you're already sleeping well, find another positive way to boost your physical energy: focus on improving your nutrition, hydration, or exercise. There are endless ways to strengthen your physical well-being. The point is that we all need to slow down and take better care of ourselves on a daily basis. And even the smallest of changes can make a significant difference in your energy and ability to communicate more effectively.

ELEVATE YOUR EMOTIONS

Take a minute and think back over your day. How many different emotions have you felt in the last hour? How about the past two or three hours? When you step back and look at your experiences you'll notice that you feel a wide range of emotions every single day: excited, grateful, worried, frustrated, guilty. All emotions are valuable in that they help us stay connected to our experiences, but not all emotions are equally helpful when it comes to how they support our well-being, relationships, and communication.

It's not surprising that scientists have discovered that our negative emotions weigh on us more heavily than positive ones. All you have to do is think back to the last time you got some bad news to appreciate how quickly negative emotions can tank your mood. But few people understand that when you dip into lower emotional states—for example when you become anxious, have feelings of regret, or blame others—it exponentially affects everything from the way you communicate to your life-view.

The pioneering research of Dr. David R. Hawkins around consciousness and emotional states led to a number of scientific breakthroughs that ultimately became what is called the Map of Consciousness. While the premise of Hawkins's work—negativity drains, positivity uplifts—is grounded in common sense, what's so powerful about it is that it quantifies the extraordinary shift in well-being that we experience when we change emotional states. The Map of Consciousness calibrates emotions on a logarithmic scale of energetic power (to the base of 10) ranging from 1 to 1,000; this means that every shift is exponential. It shows that when we move out of the vibration of fear (which calibrates at 100, or 10^{100}) and into the vibration of love (which calibrates at 500, or 10^{500}), we experience an expanded shift in energy that radically changes our emotional state. When we chose to become a loving person and have experiences that produce feelings of love or joy, our body releases endorphins, which have profound effects on our physical and emotional well-being.[12]

Most of us don't think about creating more positive emotions when we slip into negativity, but we'd be better off if we did. It can feel as though our emotions just wash over us unbidden and uncontrollable. But the truth is that we can create more positive emotions—we have the ability to lift our mood and broaden our outlook. The study of positive psychology has revealed that we can all elevate our emotions on purpose, by simply going for a five-minute walk in nature, soaking up some sunshine, watching a YouTube clip that makes us laugh, decluttering our desks, or focusing on all that's going well in our lives. We can create more endorphins and shift our mindset to direct (and redirect) our emotional state.

When we practice creating a positive mindset through the environment that we create for ourselves, the people we surround ourselves with, or encouraging self-talk, we positively charge our batteries so that we have the energy we need to be at our best. It's important to equip ourselves with a positive outlook and develop the tools to shift our mindset when fear creeps in, as it's bound to do from time to time.

For example, have you ever been nervous before a presentation, or an important conversation, and experienced how quickly fear can destabilize you? Your mind jumps to everything that might go wrong and before you know it what initially felt challenging now feels overwhelming as stress hijacks your mind and body. Suddenly you're at a loss for words. You can't remember a single point you wanted to make, and you start to stumble through without a coherent thought. In the moment, you might take a few deep breaths to regain your composure and get through the presentation, but the lingering residue of negative emotions takes a bit more clearing. Even after it's over, the feelings of nervousness and self-doubt can linger.

Research has discovered that a quick burst of positive emotions works like an antidote to negate stress and anxiety. Psychologists call it the "undoing effect." Positive emotions have the ability to neutralize our negative feelings.[13] This means you have the ability to pull yourself out of that downward spiral by deliberately creating more positive emotions. (And you don't have to wait for a difficult situation to invest in creating more positive energy!) One of the simplest, fastest things you can do after going through a challenging experience is to take a breath and think of all of the people you love and appreciate.

Breathing techniques are an extremely effective way to manage the heightened emotions and stress during intense experiences and raise our emotional state. By consciously taking several deep breaths, you direct your nervous system to stay in a calm state when stress builds. Developing this habit will also train your body to instinctually take a deep breath when the first pangs of stress or anxiety appear. The nice thing about breathing methods is that you can use them in any situation—sitting in a meeting, on a phone call, or when standing and presenting—to shift your mind, body, and emotions in an instant.

There are many, many breathing techniques and I encourage you to try a few to find what works for you. A personal favorite is a simple breathing practice that has been shown to elicit emotions of joy: Breathe in slowly and deeply through your *nose* and exhale slowly and deeply through your nose. Keep your breaths regular and balanced and relax your rib cage.[14] Give it a try the next time you're caught up in the intensity of an emotion that you'd like to move above. (Or now, if you just want to feel more joy!) The key to managing and boosting our emotional states through breathwork is to practice the techniques every day—not just when we're in the grip of a powerful emotion we'd like to release. Try linking your breathing practice to something you do every day—like checking email or social media—and intentionally practice until it becomes second nature.

• • •

If you've ever kept a gratitude journal, you already know the profound way that writing down even just three things you appreciate in your life can shift your mindset from lack to fullness. The same goes for expressing gratitude and telling someone how much they mean to you. Whether it's a quick text or handwritten card, it feels good to express appreciation.

EXERCISE: A Burst of Gratitude

Shifting your attention to a moment of gratitude is one of the fastest ways to fill your mind and body with positive emotions. Savoring positive experiences changes your brain for the better. Scientists call this experience-dependent neuroplasticity, which means you can use the power of your mind to change your brain and create a new way of seeing things. Think of it as a micro meditation to clear your mind and boost your mood.

The next time you feel stressed, take 15 seconds to think about something that you appreciate in life—being with someone you love or an experience you've enjoyed—and let those positive feelings sink into your body.

By taking just 15 seconds to stay with your new mindset, you're able to encode your new programming deep into the fabric of your mind.[15] It's amazing! In less than one minute, you can shift your mindset and lift your mood.

By actively cultivating more positive emotions, we can fill our reservoir with positive energy to draw on when conversations feel challenging. When we begin from an elevated emotional state, we're more resilient when we face adversity. This makes it easier to emotionally navigate the difficult days at work, when you know things are going to be tough. Resilience also helps you bounce back faster when negative thinking starts to take over and one thought of self-doubt sparks a million more and your mind starts spinning out of control with scenes from your worst nightmare.

BOOST YOUR MOOD

Sometimes we forget that we have the power to change how we feel and direct our mood. The trick is to know what works for you and to have a wide range of methods—from micro moments to deeper dives—that renew your energy on whatever level you need. Some of my clients need a long run to clear out negative emotions, while others feel restored just by being in nature or gardening. Music is another powerful tool for shifting your vibe. It's one of my rituals; before I present, I have a playlist that I crank on my drive to the event and it always works to put me in a good mood. I arrive feeling energized and excited. It's also what I play after conversations that were particularly difficult and leave me feeling irritated. After a few songs that heavy feeling starts to lift.

Even small doses of positive emotions can begin to lift our spirits. Beyond the immediate benefits of feeling renewed in the moment, cultivating positive emotions will set you up to experience more joy in your life. Joy takes you beyond yourself and makes you feel alive!

EXERCISE: Spiral Up!

We can all intentionally elevate our emotions. Create a list of ideas you can activate to lift your spirits and renew your energy. You'll see that even the smallest shift has the power to change everything!

Make a list of *quick-fix* ideas for those times you need an infusion of positive energy to shift your mood, so you know just what to do. Then make another with *energy-boosting* ideas to replenish your reservoir—seeing friends, hobbies, adventures—and put at least one renewal activity on your calendar each week. It's always good to have something to look forward to!

PRACTICE POSITIVE SELF-TALK

Positive emotions are essential for elevating our well-being, but they're only half the equation. Our thoughts also have an incredible impact on how we think, feel, and communicate—and they work in tandem with our emotions. As we listen to our internal dialogue we can begin to see just where our never-ending stream of thoughts is leading us—and if we don't like the direction we're heading, we can change it.

Research has shown that the average person has roughly fifty thousand thoughts, or self-talk messages, a day. It turns out that most of our inner conversations are about ourselves and that 80% of those messages are negative.[16] We criticize ourselves all day long, saying things like, *I should have said something . . . I shouldn't have said that . . . I'm too pushy . . . I'm not assertive enough . . . They think I'm too cautious . . . I should have been kinder.* The monologue goes on and on.

We're our own worst critics, and it's quite literally exhausting: Studies have shown that negative thoughts have a draining physical impact on your body. Negative thinking creates emotional states like fear, anger, anxiety, guilt, shame, and regret, which cause stress levels to increase. The body perceives stress as a danger signal and prompts your adrenal glands to release a surge of hormones, including adrenaline and cortisol. (Chronic sleep-deprivation also elevates these hormones, making us even more reactive to our negative self-talk.)

These negative thoughts can have other physical impacts as well, especially when it's a pattern of thinking. The long-term activation of the stress-response system and the overexposure to stress hormones can disrupt almost all of your body's processes. For some people it creates anxiety, stomach issues, and digestive problems. Others experience headaches, sleep problems, weight gain, and trouble concentrating. Chronic negativity can also leave people feeling dissatisfied with their lives and lead to depression. Positive thinking, on the other hand, creates positive emotions like enthusiasm, hope, peace, and confidence, which flood our brain and bodies with endorphins that help us feel calm and alert.[17]

EXERCISE: "Cancel" Your Negative Thoughts

As you go through your day, set an intention to listen to how you talk to yourself (and others). Do you focus on the negative and only the worst? Are you quick to criticize, judge, or tear yourself down? Do you think in absolutes like "always" or "never"?

Check in on your thoughts to see where you're taking yourself. If you catch yourself thinking a negative thought, say the words "Cancel! Cancel!" silently or out loud, and then consciously redirect your mind to a positive thought. Focus on something you appreciate or someone you love instead. Go back to the "Burst of Gratitude" exercise on page 119 and experience how—in just 15 seconds—you can shift your mindset.

The tenor of our inner dialogue drives our behavior, which works well for us when we're in a positive mindset. If we're feeling open and think something is possible, we're more likely to put in the effort and go for it. But if we're in a negative mindset, we're less likely to believe in ourselves, so we don't even start. If we think we're smart and able to learn new skills, we'll invest in ourselves. But if we get stuck in fear, we're unlikely to even try or, if we do, we end up sabotaging ourselves to prove we were right.

Fortunately, you can learn to listen to your thoughts and change your inner dialogue. As soon as you notice that you're being critical or thinking negatively, you can "cancel" that thought to interrupt your thinking long enough for you to choose another, more positive narrative. Noticing and intervening creates the space we need to prune the old neural circuitry and build the new neural pathways that support positive thought patterns, so they can begin to dominate the way we think and feel.

We all have more power than we've been led to believe. We have the ability to influence our well-being by honoring the needs of our body and mind. We can take care of our physical bodies to provide a foundation that combats stress and elevates our emotions. We can cultivate more positivity and become attuned to the way we talk to ourselves. And every small change we make to improve the quality of our energy begins to build tiny habits that quickly pile up and create major differences in the way we experience life.

When you recognize that you play a key role in determining your level of stress and well-being, you empower yourself to evolve and re-create who you are. Day by day, as your self-awareness and well-being become stronger, you move your autopilot setting closer and closer to your "healthy" expression. And over time, healthy can become your predominant way of being and communicating.

CHAPTER 9

Build Healthy Relationships

*O*ur desire to feel connected and belong is a deep human need. We're social creatures by nature, so it's only natural that we want to build friendships at work—especially when you consider that we often spend more time with our colleagues than our loved ones. Just as important, we're more collaborative, resourceful, and productive when we work with people we like. We want to help our friends, so we share information and look for new ways to make things work.

Developing friendships at work—the people you grab coffee with, ask for advice about an upcoming project, or look to for a reality check when you need one—is clearly linked to our health and well-being. These positive relationships protect us from stress and improve our mental, emotional, and physical health. They boost our immunity and support our body's ability to build, maintain, and repair itself.[1] Still, it's not always easy to get along with everyone we work with. You may not like someone's personality or competitive streak and so it's inevitable that there will be conflict. But it's rare that you'll find a situation where things can't at least improve.

Most people feel that their relationship problems result from other people's behaviors, but that's only half the equation. We bear responsibility for the other half and, if we're being honest, most of us have plenty to work on. The best way to start transforming our relationships with others is by seeing how we can improve our *own* communication. The truth is that whatever you're complaining about, you're also contributing to as well—at least on some level. We always play a role, whether we're creating, promoting, or allowing something to happen.

You might be surprised by how easily you can strengthen or repair a relationship by taking a closer look at your own behavior. Once you see the role you play, you're empowered to take responsibility for what you think, say, and do. Ultimately, that's the way you foster trust, respect, and honesty in your working relationships.

OWN YOUR EMOTIONS

Have you ever heard yourself say "He makes me so mad," or "She makes me feel like I'm incompetent"? Phrases like these fly out of our mouths when we get emotionally triggered by something someone said or did, but the truth is that no one can *make* you feel anything. Your emotional response is a result of your thoughts, which are a result of your subconscious programming, which goes far deeper than whatever the situation is that pushed your buttons.

The brain works in a think-feel-act cycle. When we experience something, we have a thought, which prompts the brain to release neurochemicals that create the physical expression of an emotion that we feel in our body. Most people become aware of their thoughts once they feel the emotion, which leads them to think the emotion comes first, but it's actually the other way around. When you become aware of your inner dialogue, you'll recognize that your beliefs, thoughts, or judgments are creating the emotions that drive your reactions and behaviors.[2]

While it's natural to feel upset when something sets you off, it doesn't serve you to project your emotional responses onto others. If you look below the surface, you'll find that your emotions are often tied to an unconscious belief, past experience, or old program that instilled a feeling of not being good enough. On some level, we all feel like we're not *enough* of something. Sometimes it's the pressure that comes from our family, peers, work, or society that creates self-doubt and leaves us feeling like we don't measure up. Other times, we internalize criticism that fuels our insecurities. This doesn't mean your feelings aren't valid—you can feel whatever you feel in response to a situation—but bear in mind that whoever set you off isn't to blame.

This also means you're capable of directing your thoughts, choosing your response, and managing how you feel. When we project our emotional response onto others, it can damage our relationships. No one wants to bear the brunt of your emotional issues. For example, Anne's mother was a perfectionist and found fault in everything she did. This created a lot of insecurities that she hadn't dealt with and, as an adult, Anne had a really hard time receiving any feedback on her work. She took it personally and projected her insecurities (and issues with her mother) onto her manager, often complaining, "I've done *everything* he's asked. There's just no pleasing him!" As a result, she gained a reputation for being unresponsive to input and difficult to work with.

Remember, we're capable of choosing our responses and managing how we express our emotions. The way we do that is to start recognizing the situations and behaviors that set us off, which we call triggers. What's important to understand about emotional triggers is that you're responsible for how you react and feel. Even when our triggers provoke an intense emotional reaction, and we feel our fight, flight, or freeze response kick in, we still own how we respond. We can use that quarter-second lag time to choose how we behave.

Often, our triggers were formed in childhood, when we didn't have the mental capacity or tools to deal with the situation. And so we become triggered by experiences that evoke these old, painful feelings. As adults, we can look at things more objectively and see the situation for what it was, which helps to release its hold on us.

For example, as the youngest of nine children who grew up with very vocal siblings, I was frequently cut off or drowned out when I tried to jump into a conversation. When I persisted, that desire to participate was often shut down with "What do you know?" This repeated negative experience taught me to believe that when someone interrupts me it's because they don't think what I'm saying is valuable. To this day I can still feel a pang of self-doubt when someone cuts me off. This is when I know to take a long, slow, deep breath and exhale the emotion. I've also learned to ask people to let me finish when I can tell it's an unconscious habit that's likely to persist.

For you, these triggers may be any number of different situations—someone discounting or ignoring you, someone being too busy to make time for you, or someone being judgmental or critical of you. Chances are you could easily make a list of what gets you riled up when it comes to how people communicate at work. If you've read through all the communication styles you may have already identified the aspects of the styles you love and others you could live without (forever). Most of us like people who share our styles (birds of a feather and all that), while people with other styles can rub us the wrong way. Some are annoyed by people who dive straight into business without establishing any personal connection (Expressive) and others appreciate it (Direct). Some are irritated by people who share personal stories (Reserved), while others find it critical for building relationships (Harmonious). Some feel frustrated by people who are guarded with their opinions (Expressive), and others respect that they don't overshare (Reserved). Some are bothered by people who don't speak up (Direct), and others think it's perfectly fine (Harmonious). Certainly, identifying the traits or habits that upset you is part of learning to identify your triggers, but the real work is to investigate *why*. Where does your story come from? How can dispelling that story free you to choose a different response?

It's usually painful when we feel triggered, but there's a lot we can learn from those emotions that flare up. Even if you're not the kind of person who voices their frustration in the moment, it's likely that your tone and body language are broadcasting exactly how you feel to everyone in the room. When we go to the source of what triggers us, we can gain a much clearer understanding of what sets us off, which better equips us to manage our response in real time.

For example, Jake knew he had a trigger around being on time. He became irrationally anxious if he was in danger of running late and would deliberately check his watch when someone strolled into a meeting a few minutes late to signal his disapproval. When he looked at why it bothered him so much, he realized he'd adopted his father's rigid attitude about punctuality: "If you're not early, you're late!" His father would become angry if Jake was not prepared on time; he found it disrespectful. Jake saw that he was easily triggered when his colleagues ran behind, and it caused tension when he would call them out in a way that felt shaming. It was only after he realized that his anxiety had less to do with his colleagues' perceived disrespect than his own childhood imprinting that he could take steps to mend his relationship with his team and manage his emotions.

What Triggers You?

We all have emotional triggers, but we may not always see why our triggers developed in the first place. Finding the root cause of your emotional reactions helps you to understand what makes them so powerful. If you're triggered when someone goes off on a tangent, what is it about going off-task that triggers you? Remember, our triggers originate with us—not other people. And the faster you can see that, the easier it is to manage your response and reduce your stress.

The first step is to identify what triggers an emotional reaction for you, so you can learn to see it coming. Most of us have an intuitive sense of what circumstances or behaviors cause these intense reactions, but if you find that you're struggling, read through the descriptions of *all* the communication styles and make a list of the traits you find most annoying. Remember, triggers are when you have an extreme emotional response to an experience that's disproportionate to the circumstances or how others are responding. They're usually easy to recognize because just thinking about the experience—someone trying to control you, someone who's needy, a situation where you're excluded—creates a level of discomfort and makes you lose your cool. You may even find that some of your *own* style traits can get on your nerves. Oftentimes what bothers us in others acts as a mirror so we can see ourselves more clearly. Take a closer look and see if you might exhibit that same behavior sometimes and how it might affect others.

Once you've identified your triggers, gently ask yourself *why* they're triggering for you. What's underneath them? Is there a particular memory that surfaces? Most of our triggers stem from when we were children and experienced pain and difficulties that we couldn't handle at the time. As adults, we typically get triggered by feelings that are reminiscent of our childhood wounds.

Take a look at your triggers from your adult perspective to see if you can disarm them. Sometimes when we can look at a situation with self-compassion and understanding, we can see things more clearly and release the emotional charge. The more rationally you can see the situation, the easier it is to dissolve and free yourself from your triggers.

We all have the ability to own our emotional responses and change our behavior. The faster we recognize that we're in charge of and can choose how we behave, the faster we can heal the issues that make it more difficult to get along with people and build healthy relationships at work.

CREATE POSITIVE FRIENDSHIPS

When you were young, did your mother ever try to get you to steer clear of certain friends that she could see were not the greatest influence? Well, it turns out that mothers *do* know best: we're profoundly influenced by the company we keep; the contagious behaviors of our social networks have an extraordinary impact on our well-being. Researchers at Harvard who conducted a 30+ year longitudinal study of more than 12,000 individuals found that well-being is boosted by 15% when you have a direct friendship with someone who's generally positive and happy. Not terribly surprising; we've all experienced how a friend's positive energy can uplift the way we feel.

What *was* surprising was that even indirect connections influence and boost our well-being. In other words, if your happy friend Logan has a happy friend Sam, the odds are that *your* happiness will increase by 10%, even if you don't know Sam or ever interact with him.

This positive ripple goes out another ring. If your happy friend's happy friend (Sam) also has a happy friend—let's call him Taylor—it's likely that your well-being will improve another 6%. This means that people you don't even know and never interact with directly—who are three degrees removed—can have a positive impact on your well-being.[3] You can boost your positive feelings by 31% by just by creating positive friendships.

This massive study of social networks is another illustration of how we're all connected through energetic fields that encircle us and how these connections carry energy and emotions back and forth between us that influence how we feel. The people we surround ourselves with have a significant impact on our happiness and well-being. So, in addition to taking care of our bodies, and creating opportunities to fill our positive experience reservoirs, it's also essential that we invest in building and maintaining positive relationships. Take time to nurture your work friendships—have coffee, go to lunch, take a walk—and deepen the connections that support you. Think of it as a form of self-care that boosts your emotions and keeps you in a positive space.

CULTIVATE TRUST

The quality of our relationships directly affects the quality of our work. Some people naturally excel at building trust, while others struggle to connect in a meaningful way with others. If you ever begin to feel like a work relationship is shifting in some way, it's a good idea to check in and see if you have been building or eroding trust through your actions.

It's rare that people express their feelings of distrust, largely because there has to be some level of trust to even be able to have that conversation. That's why it's all the more important that you act in trustworthy ways in all your relationships—if you maintain a high degree of integrity people will openly share ideas and information, which allows everyone to be more productive.

Trust is foundational for building healthy working relationships. When trust levels are high, communication is practically effortless. You feel safe enough to be yourself. You're open and honest with your opinions. You're willing to be vulnerable and to admit your mistakes. All these qualities deepen your connections and foster that sense of belonging that we all desire.

The way we communicate and behave heavily influences whether others see us as trustworthy or not. Do you do what you say you'll do? Do you hold confidences? Are you sincere and authentic? Are you open and approachable? Do you listen when others are speaking? Do you gossip or complain about people when they're not around? Or maybe you try to manipulate situations by being less than transparent. When you learn to take inventory of your behaviors on a daily basis, you'll see a more accurate picture of what level of trust you're creating through your interactions.

Are You Trustworthy?

There are a number of ways you can build (and lose) trust with your colleagues. Here's a quick checklist you can use to see how effectively you build trust and where your behaviors may be creating problems. As you read through each statement, give yourself a letter grade that reflects your general behavior. Then look at the relationships where you struggle to get along with people to see where you may want to be more intentional about building trust through your actions.

- Sincere—My private and public conversations align. I'm honest and authentic with people.
- Transparent—I'm open and up front with people. I don't have hidden agendas.

- Reliable—I consistently keep my commitments.
- Vulnerable—I admit if I've made a mistake and apologize if I've caused a problem.
- Respectful—I treat everyone with respect, even those I disagree with.
- Open—I invite people to share their opinion and it's okay if they disagree with me.
- Listening—I make room for others to share their perspectives and give them my full attention when they're talking.

You can use this checklist every day to evaluate how your behaviors are impacting your working relationships. It only takes a few minutes to strengthen your self-awareness, which is the first step toward all positive change!

Every interaction is an opportunity to connect, build relationships, and nurture trust. And when you intentionally and proactively behave in ways that build trust, you can strengthen even the most difficult relationships.

STAY ABOVE THE LINE

There's a thin line that separates our behavior from the level of accountability we take for our actions: on one side we take responsibility for how we communicate, and on the other we don't. If it sounds simple, that's because it is. And in its simplicity lies its strength.

This concept stems from a behavioral model called "above the line and below the line," which originated with organizational culture expert Carolyn Taylor's classic book *Walking the Talk*, which spread the model worldwide.[4] The "line" in this model represents *choice*. It's based on the idea that no matter what you're experiencing, the one aspect you have within your control is how you choose to respond. We choose whether we operate above the line, meaning we accept personal responsibility, or below it, where we prefer to deflect, ignore, or blame factors outside our control to justify our behavior.

The simplicity of the design makes it easy to understand. When you operate above the line, you're open, curious, and positive. You own your emotions, behaviors, and experiences—and just as important, you're able to learn from them. On the other hand, when you fall below the line your focus is on protecting yourself, which means you're likely to make excuses, blame, or complain. Alternately, you may attack others, withdraw, or ignore the situation entirely. The fastest way to erode trust is to operate below the line.

Have you ever noticed how when one person steps up and owns something that went wrong at work—or didn't achieve the results intended—others step in to share the accountability? This is especially true when you work in teams. It only takes one person to say, "It's clear to me now, I just didn't see it at the time. Here's what I'd recommend we do differently next time" to inspire others to do the same. We're all self-leaders and when we choose to operate above the line, we're able to learn and grow through our experiences—and encourage others to do the same.

Sometimes our response patterns become so conditioned that we don't even realize how we're behaving or coming across to others. However, through intentional practice and reflection, we can become more aware of what we're thinking, feeling, and doing. That's the whole point of this exercise: to learn to see ourselves more clearly and recognize the signs that tell us we're in danger of slipping below the line, so we can *choose* to communicate intentionally, build trust, and reduce stress.

Above- and Below-the-Line
Communication Behaviors

Responsible for what you say and do

Sincere, honest

Trustworthy

Listen actively

Open, positive

Engaged and curious

Patient

Empathetic, compassionate

Transparent

Respectful

Defuse tension

Resolve conflicts

Blame

Complain

Gossip, inauthentic

Passively listen, tune out

Negative, closed

Judgmental, shaming

Interrupt, disrespectful

Disagreeable, argumentative

Insincere, dishonest

Manipulate, control

Ignore tension

Avoid conflict

Stay Above the Line

Once you start paying attention to your actions, you may be surprised by how often you slip below the line. Don't judge yourself too harshly—we all fall below the line more often when we first begin monitoring our behavior, and recognizing it puts you on the path to growth. In fact, every time you can see your behavior and choose a better response give yourself a pat on the back as a little positive reinforcement. It's important to acknowledge and appreciate your progress.

We can only change what we're willing to see and the more you look the faster you'll see it and be able to course correct. Remember, your thoughts and emotions precede your words and behaviors, so choosing to stay above the line is much easier when you're mindful of what you're thinking and feeling.

Each day, choose and commit to one above-the-line behavior from the list on page 134. Notice any time you feel yourself wanting to slip below the line, and get curious about that behavior: *Why am I wanting to behave this way? What am I thinking and feeling? What impact will this have on my working relationships if I continue down this path?* Then redirect your response toward that above-the-line behavior. At first you may become aware that you dipped below the line well after the fact. However, as your practice becomes established, you'll keep making progress. And one day you'll find you're at the point where you can hear your thoughts before they become emotions and choose your behavior with ease.

Pause for a moment at the end of the day to check in on your behavior. You can use the "above and below the line" checklist as a simple reflection tool to see where your behaviors landed. Be objective and thorough *and* remember to celebrate moments where you stayed above the line too—our negative experiences weigh more heavily on us, which means that one tough moment can overshadow several positive experiences in a day. Commit to this practice for at least a week to stay mindful of your behavior and more firmly establish it in your routine.

Remember, no matter what you're experiencing, the one aspect that you have within your control is how you respond. As your consciousness rises, you'll find that being accountable feels much better than avoiding responsibility. It's truly empowering!

CLEAR THE AIR

No matter how much we love our jobs or the people we work with, disagreements will happen from time to time. The reality is that work can feel overwhelming, people can become competitive, and stress rarely brings out the best in anyone. We avoid office tension hoping the disagreement will blow over, or we gossip with our friends and complain about our colleagues to get it "out of our system." We've all done it. And it's understandable—it's uncomfortable dealing with issues head-on, and it's even *more* uncomfortable to admit that we're part of the problem.

The trouble is that if we leave issues unaddressed they're likely to snowball into situations that are even more challenging to deal with. We ruminate, replaying the situation over and over in our minds—which only further stirs up our emotions and drains our energy. If tensions begin to brew between you and someone you work with, the best thing you can do is clear the air.

Let's be clear: This isn't a moment to air grievances, or to confront a colleague about their behavior. Clearing the air is about taking responsibility for your *own* actions and addressing moments where your behavior caused (or added to) the stress between you. Did you dip below the line? Did a style gap create the irritation? Or maybe you made an assumption that caused a strain in your relationship? Once you have identified the cause, take responsibility for your behavior and acknowledge how what you said or did made matters worse. A simple apology can go a long way!

Oftentimes we don't even try to have the conversation because we're afraid of how the other person will respond. But more often than not, when you own your role and behavior others do as well. Your willingness to have the conversation could resolve your differences and repair—and even strengthen—the relationship. And even if you don't walk away with the air as clear as you'd like it to be, you can go about your day knowing that you have tried to take responsibility for making things better. Wouldn't you rather be known as someone who tries to resolve problems than someone who hides from them?

Keep in mind that how you behave shapes the way people view you. In large part, your reputation is based on your character—your level of integrity, how you treat people, your level of sincerity, and whether you take responsibility for your actions. And your character is foundational to building trusted relationships. This doesn't mean you need to be perfect or that experiencing interpersonal tensions will tank your career. In fact, when you actively try to make a difficult situation better, people will respect you more. Nordstrom is a perfect example: Its sterling reputation for customer service wasn't built by being perfect; it was built by taking responsibility for the mistakes their employees made while serving their customers. If something went wrong (which it inevitably did, since we're all human) the company did whatever it took to make it right. This behavior has made Nordstrom one of the world's most respected and admired brands. Just think of what taking more responsibility for your relationships could do for your own reputation!

TIPS FOR CLEARING THE AIR

If you're catching a problem before it becomes a major issue, they're usually fairly easy to resolve. That said, when you're planning to have a "clear the air" conversation there are a few things you want to keep in mind. First, wait until you're feeling calm—but don't wait too long. Issues that are put off tend to fester. Next, have the conversation face-to-face whenever possible so you can see how they're responding. Your sincerity will come through faster in person, then in a text or email. Finally, and perhaps most important, listen to what they have to say.

If you're unsure of where to begin, you might try something like

Hey, do you have a second? I noticed/felt [describe your perspective without judgment] during our [situation: meeting, conversation, one-on-one], and I wanted to clear the air. I [describe your behavior—be specific!], and I could have handled things better. I didn't mean to [describe the impact that you perceive you had on them], and I'm sorry.

The key is to concretely and clearly describe your behavior and name the friction or discomfort you felt it caused in the relationship. Use statements that begin with "I" to make it clear that you're speaking from your perspective—your feelings, reactions, and experience—and not based on any beliefs or judgments you may have made about the other person or situation. And be genuine! Remember, people feel your intentions, so be sincere or you'll make matters worse.

We all feel tension in our working relationships at some point, even with the people we enjoy. If we allow issues to go unresolved, we lose three of our most valuable resources: time, energy, and reputation. Common sense will tell you that if you're willing to stay open and address tensions early, you'll experience fewer conflicts down the road.

RESOLVE YOUR CONFLICTS

It's inevitable that you'll experience conflict at work, especially when time is short and stress is high. If you work with humans there will eventually be conflict—and if you constantly avoid addressing tensions when they're small, you'll have an avalanche to contend with. The fact that there will be conflict isn't the problem. The problem is our tendency to go below the line and ignore the situations we don't want to deal with. Studies have shown that 70% of employees say they deal with difficult conversations with their boss, colleagues, and direct reports by avoiding them.[5] This means we don't talk about issues that affect performance, we don't acknowledge broken promises, or we don't address mismanaged expectations. What we fail to realize is that any below-the-line behaviors that we don't discuss will simply continue to resurface and grow, which ultimately drives our stress up and well-being down. Addressing conflict goes far beyond just "getting along"—it has a direct impact on our ability to do our best work, feel safe, and communicate effectively.

At some point we all have to deal with conflict at work, and while no one enjoys difficult conversations, how we handle it varies depending on our communication style. Expressives are *by far* the most willing to step in and address tensions when conflict arises; they like to resolve things quickly. Both Directs and Reserveds will deal with conflict when they have to—and it's usually when the work begins to suffer. Otherwise, they're likely to sit back and let things play out. And Harmonious people avoid conflict whenever they can; they're extremely uncomfortable when conflict arises. All styles have the ability to step into difficult conversations; it's a communication skill that we can all learn. It's really just a matter of how quickly we address the issues and how much discomfort we feel.

Even the best communicators experience tensions at work. For example, Emma (Direct) was known for being responsible, producing quality work, and meeting deadlines. She often had suggestions that would raise the quality of the team's work and Brian had started taking advantage of her input. When he was juggling multiple projects he gave less attention to his work with Emma, knowing she'd pull it together in the clutch. During internal reviews he would share ideas that were "still taking shape" and far from client-ready. Emma didn't want to address the real issue (i.e., that Brian was taking advantage of her), so she would flesh out the ideas and get them packaged for presentation—she saved him time and again, and he knew it. This had become their pattern, and it was one that was creating a lot of stress and frustration for Emma.

Rather than staying below the line and continuing to avoid the situation, Emma chose to have a conversation with Brian at the outset of their next assignment. Her intention was to reduce the stress this dynamic was creating, rebuild trust, and deliver great work for their clients. Knowing that Brian was Reserved, she knew he'd care that his behavior was affecting their relationship and impacting the team. She used a recent example—where he'd shown up unprepared and she helped finish his work—acknowledging that she had allowed it to keep happening. She told him that she was already worried about this project and the stress was becoming too much. She outlined her needs and expectations and told him she wouldn't be there to help him the next time—he was responsible for his portion of the assignment. It was a turning point for Brian, who realized the full impact of his behavior and started taking responsibility for *all* of his work.

Learning to address conflict when tensions arise or issues persist will make a significant difference in your relationships and well-being. It takes courage to step into the conversation and intentional practice to say things in a way that help people to stay open, see what's transpiring, and hear what needs to change.

STEPPING INTO DIFFICULT CONVERSATIONS

Learning to effectively address conflict is a skill that we can all develop. Here is a simple process you can use to step into the conversation more purposefully to put people at ease while being clear about what you'd like to see improve. The more you prepare, the better you'll be able to communicate your needs, listen to others, and work toward a resolution.

Identify the core issue. Anytime you're feeling stuck in a pattern of persistent issues and tension, ask yourself the following questions: What conversation is needed? What are we not addressing that's keeping us stuck here? What do I want for the relationship? What do I need to get out of this conversation? What needs to change?

Acknowledge your role. We always play a role and it usually involves a below-the-line behavior (p. 134). Take a clear and honest look at how you have been contributing to the situation and what you can do differently to help resolve things.

Understand their communication style. Try to empathize with their perspective. Sometimes misunderstandings lead to conflicts that are a result of different approaches to communicating. When you're familiar with their communication style, you'll recognize if they begin to shift into their style under stress.

Focus on the facts. Be calm, clear, and kind as you share your perspective. Keep your comments grounded in facts as you share your point of view. Acknowledge how you have contributed to the situation. Explain how you have been feeling. Watch for any emotions that surface and keep breathing, so you remain calm.

Stay open and curious. Listen to their perspective with an open mind. Listen empathetically and employ all of your senses. Ask questions to clarify and watch for making assumptions or judgments. Look for the subtle cues and body language that indicate how they're feeling.

Come to an agreement. Be sure you're both clear about how you'll resolve the issue. End with clear expectations around any shifts in behavior that are needed. And agree to check back in to see how things are going in a week or two.

We all have the ability to choose a new response and create new outcomes. We just need to be willing to have the conversations that are needed. And we must be willing to allow people to change. Remember, our brains see what we tell them to look for (confirmation bias), so intentionally look for the positive changes you're hoping to see in others. If we only look for the qualities in people that we've been conditioned to expect, once we see even a hint of old behaviors, our brain will confirm that they haven't changed and stop gathering information. People are inherently good, so give others the benefit of the doubt and actively look for the best in them.

• • •

What's more difficult—and also more powerful—is to work on our own growth and development. We all participate in and contribute to creating the issues that affect the quality of our relationships and the quality of our work. If we want things to change, *we* need to be willing to change.

We're all capable of growing and shifting how we interact. We can become more aware of what triggers us and learn to choose how we respond. We can intentionally cultivate positive friendships and build trust. And we can learn to address interpersonal tensions and conflicts to eliminate some of the stress we feel. There's so much that we can do to positively impact our relationships and foster the sense of belonging we all crave.

It's hard to overstate the importance of human connection. We have the ability to uplift one another, boosting our levels of joy, health, productivity, and resilience. And yet it's easy to take this for granted and allow our egos, emotions, and insecurities to create barriers between us. The good news is that we also have the power to remove these barriers by taking more responsibility for how we show up and the impact we have on people. We have the ability to create a positive impact in our working environment and find more meaning through our work. Life is infinitely easier when we learn to get out of our own way.

Now that you know how to recognize and care for your physical, emotional, and mental health it's time to put these practices into action. It's not enough to know what to do, you need to *use* what you know. If you want to feel more purpose, meaning, and satisfaction in your work, you have to actively strengthen your foundation of well-being. There are so many ways you can improve your well-being—pick one and get started! Then, repeat daily and keep building. When we level up our well-being, we level up the quality of our communication, the quality of our relationships, and the quality of the impact we have on the world around us!

Part 4

Flex Your Communication Style

CHAPTER 10

Elevate Your Approach

*I*magine how much easier every day would be if each of us took a moment to consider how to successfully communicate with others: You recognize a coworker feeling anxious over a new assignment and slow down the discussion to give them time to ask questions. In the weekly staff meeting you notice people watching the clock and pull the conversation back around to work. You feel your body tense up after a colleague's comment and take a deep breath so you can calmly respond. Knowing your team has been feeling disconnected as they work remotely, you create time for personal connections before diving into the work.

Just think about how much more smoothly every interaction would go if we were to consider the needs and preferences of others and be flexible with our style so people feel at ease. This is what elevated communicators do: they make a few temporary adjustments to how they approach a conversation, and it makes all the difference in the world.

On some level we all naturally know how to adapt to the communication preferences of others. You have a colleague who likes to be in charge, and so you let them lead. You work on a team where people are more formal, and so you eliminate personal chitchat and stay focused. You give people time to air ideas when they're excited about a potential direction.

When we're in the healthy expression of our style, we're better at sensing what people need and more gracious in meeting those needs. You realize your manager is feeling pressured and so you quicken your pace to match the urgency you hear in their tone. When a colleague is struggling with how to approach a situation you take time to listen and help them think things through. Or when a team member is hesitant to share their ideas you make it easier for them to join the conversation. Remove the stress of a deadline, or the anxiety of a crushing workload, and we're much more considerate in our interactions with people; we're happy to bend.

But when the pressure is on, we tend to operate from the autopilot and stressed expressions of our style. When we're faced with a scarcity of resources, emotional bandwidth, or time, we focus on meeting our own needs first. We become more rigid and irritable. The urgency of our manager feels more like they're pushing us. The struggles of a colleague test our patience. The reluctance of a coworker to speak up becomes annoying. Sometimes we internalize our frustrations, and other times we let them be known. But the truth is they're always "known." We feel what others feel and we hear what goes unsaid; our energy fields are always broadcasting our thoughts and emotions, even when we think we aren't letting on. Our silence creates an undercurrent that erodes trust—one that pulls us further and further out to sea as we replay a conversation and ruminate over whatever injustice we've created in our minds.

FLEXING YOUR STYLE

It's not always easy to get along with everyone you work with, but it's worth trying. Good interpersonal skills are correlated with higher degrees of resiliency, productivity, and satisfaction.[1] It's a skill we can all learn, and it's called *flexing your style*: Temporarily adjusting the way you express yourself by leaning toward another person's communication needs and preferences. Sometimes it's as easy as finding similarities between your primary and secondary styles that help you to sync up. Other times, flexing requires more deliberate shifts in behavior when there's a larger gap between your style preferences.

Flexing your style is actually pretty simple. All it takes is a bit more intention and patience with people whose needs are different from yours. All styles have the ability to get along well. When style conflicts create people problems it's more about being inflexible rather than irreconcilable differences. People with different styles work well together all time. It may require a little flexibility, ideally on both sides, but even if you're the only one flexing, you can create positive interactions.

For example, as a consultant Mike (Direct) became adept at flexing to all kinds of people and styles; he knew that when it was easy for his clients to relate to him even the most difficult conversations would go more smoothly. He managed projects across departments where personality issues and information silos were common. While he would prefer to get right down to business, he learned to soften his Direct approach and take a few minutes to check in and see how people were doing before starting a meeting. Through this simple adjustment, he created an environment where people felt comfortable and could be themselves. As the team became more connected, trust was established, and they shared information more openly, which got the work moving faster. Ultimately, people were able to focus on work issues rather than interpersonal ones.

We all have the ability to elevate our approach and intentionally flex our style. We can positively influence the outcomes by shifting how we approach conversations. There are very few things we can control in life, but how we engage, behave, and respond is well within our control. That doesn't mean it's always easy, especially if you're feeling pressured, emotionally triggered, or depleted, but it *is* possible to develop this skill.

You may be surprised by how making just a few temporary adjustments can dramatically improve your relationships, reduce your stress, and help you accomplish more. If you're thinking, "Why should I always have to be the one to flex?" keep in mind that flexing isn't only about accommodating the other person, it's about making your own life easier. When you're willing to flex, you improve your working relationships and reduce the number of interpersonal issues that cause stress. This means you have the ability to increase your productivity and enjoy your work more. The investment you make through flexing your style allows everyone to be at their best more often—including you.

FLEXING: WHAT IT IS AND WHAT IT ISN'T

Flexing your style is about making a few temporary behavioral adjustments to the way you communicate in order to intentionally put the other person at ease. The idea is to make people feel comfortable so they can just be themselves. When people feel comfortable, they're more likely to open up and tell you what they're really thinking; and honest conversations—where people share concerns and raise issues—can dramatically improve the quality of your work *and* the quality of your relationships. The more positive interactions you have, the more trust you build and the more forthcoming people become. And trust opens the door to genuine connections and meaningful conversations.

People who work on teams or in cultures where trust is low rarely feel safe enough to share what they're actually thinking and feeling. It's only when they have nothing to lose that their walls come down. Have you ever noticed how open people become once they've given their two-week notice? When they no longer feel the pressure to conform, or fear retribution, people don't hold back; they share perspectives and opinions they didn't feel comfortable enough to voice before. Generally, their insights are extremely valuable and would have been more helpful to the organization if they'd been shared much earlier. Imagine how much better work would be if every everyone—from the leaders to those on the front lines—flexed to the needs of others so everyone felt more at ease and worked together to create a culture filled with openness and trust. Flexing your style holds this potential.

Flexing isn't about changing your personality; it's about changing your approach. Ideally, you shift your behavior at the beginning of the conversation to create alignment. Then you slide back into your own natural style so that it doesn't feel manipulative. And to be clear, flexing is *never* about manipulation or control. There are ethical differences between flexing to influence others versus flexing to create mutually beneficial interactions. If there's a hidden agenda behind a style flex, it will ultimately work against you. Remember, people can feel your intentions, and when they become aware of the manipulation, you can bet they'll be angry and any trust you had between you will be damaged.

Flexing is all about building better relationships when style tensions are getting in the way. The idea is to get off to a strong start by reducing the friction that style differences can stir up. You'll be amazed at how a few simple shifts in behavior—listening, pacing, body language, assertiveness, the amount of airtime you use—can create more positive connections.

For example, styles that naturally speak slowly and deliberately frustrate those who prefer a quick tempo. The reverse holds true as well. You've got people who love to tell stories and provide a lot of context and others who like to get straight to the point. One style isn't better than another—they're just different. *Flexing is about bridging our style differences so that we can effectively communicate with all kinds of people.*

Now, some people confuse flexing their style with needing to change their perspective. Keep in mind that flexing is about temporary *behavioral* changes; it's not about changing what you think or believe. It's not about watering down your opinion, or avoiding difficult conversations, or changing the content or goals of your conversation in any way. In fact, you're more likely to create distrust if you're not honest about what you believe. Your aim is to tailor your approach so that people hear your thoughts and ideas without biases or judgment based on your delivery. Removing style irritations allows you to create an environment where people are more receptive, which is quite helpful when you know you hold different perspectives or need to discuss difficult issues.

> Flexing your style is about making two or three temporary behavioral adjustments to the way you communicate in order to intentionally put the other person at ease.

ALL CHANGE STARTS WITH YOU

Everyone has the ability to flex their style to improve their relationships, but not everyone uses it. Sometimes we fail to see that we contribute to the communication problems we experience. Instead, we complain and gossip about the people who annoy us. We find fault in their behavior, wish they would change, and dread having to deal with people who rub us the wrong way. When we recognize that our own behavior is contributing to the problem, we have the ability to change our contribution to make things better. The biggest hurdle to improving communication is often our own willingness to change and put the needs of others ahead of our own. But if you can learn to flex beyond your own preferences, you'll find that you're able to communicate effectively with almost anyone.

It's much easier to build rapport with different styles when you shift how you approach a conversation. It usually only takes a couple of minor adjustments to get in sync and create more ease in your exchanges. Experience has proven you'll be more successful and effective if you focus on just one or two modifications at a time. You don't want to flex too much, or for too long, or you'll come across as insincere and pandering. People will start questioning your sincerity and motives. Done well, flexing should be nearly invisible.

I'd been coaching for Kim for a few months and hearing about how difficult she found working with Nick. He was about as direct and succinct as they come when engaging with others at work. Meanwhile Kim was highly expressive: she loved to think out loud, tell stories about her weekend, and build personal relationships. The biggest point of friction for them was in meetings. Nick's approach to meetings was get in, get going, and get back to work. Kim, on the other hand, loved to use meetings to explore new ideas and deepen her connection with her team. If Kim let the conversation stray into personal territory, Nick was visibly irritated, and it negatively affected the whole team. Rather than trying to get Nick to change, Kim took the initiative and started flexing to meet his needs. She made it a point to start the meeting right on time, stay focused on business, and wrap up five minutes early. Anyone who wanted to talk afterward could stick around, and those who wanted to leave were free to go. All it took were a few simple adjustments to eliminate the friction between their styles.

The biggest hurdle in improving communication is often our own willingness to change and put the needs of others ahead of our own.

WHEN FLEXING MATTERS MOST

Flexing your communication style is critical when the stress is high. Stress naturally puts us in a defensive posture and we become more rigid, which rarely makes things better. Have you ever worked for a boss who went into overdrive when they were feeling stressed? They pick up the pace and bulldoze through conversations, unable to see the damage left in their wake. When people around you are exhibiting signs of their style under stress, it's a good idea to flex your style toward theirs to avoid creating any additional tension.

It's also helpful to intentionally flex your style when you're stepping into a difficult conversation. When you start out on the same wavelength as the other person it helps them feel safe, which makes even the most challenging conversations easier. You'll want to watch for signs of tension or lack of safety throughout the conversation and look for ways to naturally flex to accommodate their needs in the moment (more on that in a minute!).

FLEXING UP, DOWN, AND ACROSS

There are certain working relationships and situations where we naturally flex our communication style. Most of us, for example, have been taught to manage up, since those relationships are key to our advancement. Once you identify your manager's style, you make it a point to act in ways that align with their strongest preferences to see what puts them at ease and what irritates them. Typically, people will let you know—directly or indirectly—so take note. And if you can't figure them out, find the right moment to ask about their preferences and pet peeves, so you can mirror the traits they love and eliminate those they don't.

One of the most overlooked relationships when it comes to flexing is with the people we manage. In part, this is because cultural norms have conditioned us to believe that everyone is supposed to manage up, and so we expect the same in return: you cater to your boss's style, so your staff should cater to yours. You'll find, though, that true leaders take the needs of their team into account. If they have someone on their team who likes to tell stories, they let them tell their stories. If someone likes to keep things brief, they honor that need and wrap things up quickly. People are happiest and most productive when they can move to their own beat. As long as it doesn't get in the way, why not accommodate their needs?

Flexing toward your peers may prove to be the most challenging, given that many of us have been trained to think of people at our level as our competition. This is one of the most important mindsets we need to shift if we want to reduce interpersonal tension, increase well-being, and have a positive impact at work. Remember, flexing has the ability to improve your relationships, reduce your stress, and strengthen productivity. Your willingness to put someone else at ease is actually a win-win. Given the growing importance of collaboration, the people who have the ability and skills to build high-functioning teams today are going to be the leaders of tomorrow.

When we intentionally flex and prioritize the communication needs of our teams and colleagues, we're sure to see the return on that investment in the quality of our relationships. And all that it requires is that we spend a little time trying to understand what they need so we're more effective in our approach. The upside is that flexing naturally moves us toward the healthiest expression of our style; it helps to bring out the best in all of us.

CHAPTER 11

Make It a Practice

*L*ike all skills, learning to flex your communication style takes intentional practice. At first, it may feel uncomfortable or foreign to you, but with time and practice it will become more natural. You simply go through the flexing steps and prepare to create a positive connection. It may seem odd that you need to prepare for a conversation, but the reality is we do it all the time. We think through how to sell in an idea as we walk the dog. We run through how a conversation might flow as we drive to work. We plan out meetings and build agendas. We strategically bring up sensitive topics when we know people are most receptive. When coaching a direct report, we consider how to best share insights and provide direction. The reason we rehearse is because it works—the time we invest preparing makes us more effective. And it's no different when it comes to flexing your style.

The more you practice flexing, the faster it will become second nature. You'll quickly identify a person's communication style as you're interacting with them. You'll recognize how they like to operate and become aware of their dominant style preferences. As your insights into others expand, you'll find that you can flex your style in the moment without a lot of planning. Until then, you'll want to follow the design for establishing your practice to build this skill.

IDENTIFYING COMMUNICATION STYLES

When we've worked with someone for a long time, it's relatively easy to identify their communication style. But even if you don't have a lot of history working together, observing how people interact in meetings, how they come across in casual conversations, or even how they write emails will usually provide you with enough information to go on. Each style has several clear "tells" that become more obvious when you pay attention to how people interact with you and others in *everyday* working situations. How we show up, day in and day out, is more reflective of our style than, say, a high-stakes meeting or new business pitch where people are likely to be "on." This is why paying attention to everyday interactions is more likely to provide you with accurate insights.

When you communicate with people, watch to see how they show up most of the time: Are they talkative, more on the quiet side, or somewhere in the middle? Do they like to lead, sit back and participate, or do they need to be drawn out? Do they speak fast, slow, or somewhere in between? Do they get straight to the point or like to tell stories? Do they step into conflict or wait for others to address challenging situations? Do they reveal their feelings or are they more private with their emotions? All of these communication traits provide clues.

Once you have a good sense of how someone typically behaves, use the Communication Style Assessment (TheElevatedCommunicator.com) and answer the questions according to the behavior you've observed to determine their primary style. Then read through their profile to see if it fits how you perceive them. Remember, they don't need to exhibit every trait in order for the style to be accurate. What you're looking for are predominant themes that best reflect their behaviors.

How to Recognize Communication Styles

	Expressive	Reserved	Direct	Harmonious
Distinctive Traits	Talkative, high energy, assertive, tells stories	Confident, team player, very professional	Gets to the point, candid, prepared, results oriented	Quieter, good listener, supportive, tentative
Pace	Fast	Steady	Brisk	Slower
Body Language	Animated, big gestures	Few gestures, controlled	Limited, pointed	Small gestures
Decision-Making	Collaborative	Wants to influence	Independent	Consultative
Conflict Management	Steps into it	Sits back	Addresses when needed	Actively avoids
Value	Working in teams	Having influence	Being responsible	Keeping the peace

CLOSING STYLE GAPS

It may seem obvious, but clearly identifying the gaps between your style and the style of the person you're communicating with is an essential first step to flexing. There are a number of ways you can work to bridge style gaps and sync up with someone and we'll talk about those in a minute, but the most successful flex will be the one that addresses the communication dynamic(s) that create the most friction. If you can identify the needs of the person you're communicating with, you can flex toward them. It's that simple!

Let's take David as an example. As an Expressive, David loved to share personal stories to kick off team meetings. He thought that the more he revealed about his life the closer his team would feel to him, but it had the exact opposite effect. His team was filled with Reserved and Direct styles who found it unprofessional and a waste of time but were uncomfortable saying anything, and since he was the CEO there was no way they were going to address it. Once he became aware of the style gap, he kept his meetings focused on work and saved his stories for informal gatherings. He found that the less he talked, the more engaged his team became. Their interactions were more productive, their relationships more trusting, and the palpable awkwardness of the meetings evaporated. Everyone started operating at a higher level, which resulted in more billable hours and less stress for everyone, especially David.

It helps to have a good sense of self-awareness when you're trying to identify what communication behaviors to focus on modifying. As you select the strategies that will make your style flex most effective, you may find it helpful to go back and revisit the insights you gained in Chapter 7. If you find it difficult to accurately see yourself (we all have blind spots!), try asking someone you trust for feedback to help you identify what you might be missing.

With your own style tendencies in mind, read through the style description of the other person (see Part 2 for communication styles), looking specifically for the areas where your styles *differ*. Those are your gaps. The next chapter, "Bridging Style Gaps," provides specific actions for each style based on the most common style differences between your style and others. In the meantime, there are a number of techniques that are important to understand so you can be effective when flexing your style.

Communicating with Someone of Your Own Style

For the most part, we enjoy and easily sync up with people who share our style; however, if we're too alike, our dominant characteristics can begin to push against one another. For example, two Reserved people may find it difficult to compromise if they're both looking to exert their influence. Put a couple of Expressives together and they may enjoy the discussion but find they ran out of time before they were able to make a decision. If you find that you're struggling to communicate with someone who shares your style, instead of focusing on the gaps, reflect instead on the dominant characteristics you share, and where you notice that you may have too much of a good thing.

START SMALL AND BUILD

Flexing works best when you modify just a few behaviors to close the biggest gaps between your styles. Select one to three strategies that you feel you can easily handle and start small. Test-drive a couple to see how well they work. You'll get more immediate feedback if you can apply them in a face-to-face interaction such as a meeting or one-on-one conversation, but you can also try flexing on phone calls, in emails, or in texts/instant messages. (If people like brevity they're going to appreciate it in every form of communication.) Flexing is effective no matter how you're communicating; it can just be a little harder to understand how people are responding to your efforts when you can't fully see or read their reaction, so you'll want to listen closely for how things are going.

If you find that your style adjustments are working well—better connection, more openness, higher productivity—look for additional ways to get on the same wavelength. And if you're not seeing any real improvement, experiment a bit to see if you've found the real issue that's creating tension.

A note of caution: Watch for overflexing! Some people are too eager to change their behavior and go all in. This approach can and will backfire. Switching your style too drastically can feel manipulative or controlling. It's important to be yourself and genuine.

Always remember, flexing is a *temporary* behavioral change. Don't feel that you need to overhaul the way you communicate all the time—strategic, brief flexes will keep rapport high and facilitate more productive, trusting conversations. When you start to flex your style, you'll find that you'll maximize your efforts if you focus on these key strategies.

Get Off to a Positive Start

Have you ever noticed how much easier it is to interact with others when you feel like you've hit a good groove? When we can find that flow at the beginning of a conversation our connections tend to be easier and more productive. This is why flexing can be most effective when you use it to align with the other person at the outset of your interaction. A couple of style adjustments usually go a long way to create synergy between people. After a few minutes of flexing, gradually ease back into your own style so it feels more natural for you, while paying attention to the interpersonal dynamics. If you start to sense tension building, look for ways to be more flexible in your approach.

Have Strong (Re)Flexes

We've all been in conversations that start out well but take a turn for the worse. Sometimes they take a sharp turn that comes out of nowhere, like when someone gets triggered and has a big reaction you didn't see coming. Other times it's like going around a slow bend where you can feel the conversation pulling in a direction that's not going to end well. Learning to listen for the cues that signal style irritation or resistance will allow you to flex in the moment and keep the conversation on track.

Andrea could always tell when tension was in the air and had come to recognize everyone's signature "tell" on her leadership team. The CEO would begin to cut people off. The COO pushed his chair back to create physical distance, and the CMO ramped up her pace to plow through. She had a flex response for each that quickly reset the direction: She asked the CEO a question so she could say what was on her mind, she cut right to the chase to pull the COO back in, and matched the pace of the CMO to keep things moving. Those small flexes kept the peace and protected their relationships.

Flexing can also help preserve relationships when a conversation has completely derailed. For example, Dan (an Expressive) was griping about a coworker, and it triggered Jane (Harmonious), who completely shut down. Gossiping set her off. Instantly, Dan realized his mistake. He wanted to fix things then and there, but knew she needed some time. So, he waited a day to circle back around to apologize for venting and promised not to do it again. Jane could feel his sincerity, and they had a productive conversation that led to a deeper connection.

Flexing in the Moment

Flexing in real time allows you to address unforeseen situational needs. Practice staying mindful and listen for the subtle cues that signal tension in a conversation, such as a shift in tone or body language. Pay attention to your instinctual reaction, take a deep breath, and hit pause as you exhale. Instead of leading with your style, choose a response that supports the other person. Ask yourself, "What do they need?" Then adjust your behavior and respond in a way that will put them at ease.

Check In

Every flexing experience holds insights into what's working and what's not. Mental check-ins during the conversation allow you to flex in the moment and recognize how your behavioral shifts are landing. Periodically, you'll also want to do a more thorough check-in to evaluate how things are going, especially after an important meeting or difficult conversation.

The easiest reflection technique is to ask yourself two basic questions: "What's working?" and "What's not?" These questions help you to see how effective your approach has been. I highly recommend that you write your answers out on paper. This helps you to see things more clearly and provides a reference piece you can come back to before your next encounter.

If you want to dig a little deeper:

Start by reflecting back on the conversation and noting what went well . . .

- What style adjustments in your behavior created more ease?
- How did your connection improve?
- What made it so effective?

Next, look at what didn't work as well as you'd hoped . . .

- What style adjustments fell flat or had no discernable impact?
- Why didn't it work? Was it the wrong approach? What was the problem?
- What would you do differently now?

By stepping outside of your experience and witnessing the exchange from an observer's perspective, you can start to see more objectively how you might create more positive connections. People and communication are complex! When you take the time to invest in learning how to nuance your approach, you'll be far more successful. The better you understand what motivates someone, or what they need, the more easily you can flex your approach.

Flexing your style is a powerful technique that you can learn to master through practice. The more consistently you flex to meet the needs of others, the more consistently you improve the quality of your relationships. And the quality of your relationships affects your level of well-being, productivity, and positive impact.

CHAPTER 12

Bridging Style Gaps

*W*e all have our own preferred ways of communicating, and sometimes we luck into a rhythm of interaction with people where everything flows. You find a kindred spirit, and you hit a good rhythm where there's a natural give-and-take that's both productive and enjoyable. It's like a dance, where each of you moves with ease and grace. Other conversations, though, can feel forced—you're stepping on each other's toes, completely off beat, which leaves you both feeling agitated. These missteps are often where our communication styles are out of sync; where we have a significant gap—or difference—in how we prefer to express ourselves or approach a situation.

The design of this chapter is intended to provide you with specific ideas to shift your style to help you communicate more effectively. Remember, flexing means making *temporary behavioral changes* in order to foster more productive working relationships with all kinds of people. Most of the strategies can be used to close style gaps and get on the same page from the outset, so you can have a more productive conversation with fewer style tensions and misunderstandings.

While each communication style has its preferred way of engaging with others, there are also several shared traits between the styles that provide common ground to build on. As you factor in the qualities of your secondary style, you're likely to find that many of the suggested shifts in behavior are easy to make. The adjustments that tend to be more challenging are frequently those where you experience style gaps that create tension points between you and your coworkers, and where flexing requires an intentional approach. In other words, you'll need to flex the most where your natural communication preferences are at odds with one another—one likes to tell stories and the other likes brevity, one speaks cautiously and the other speaks candidly. Style modifications in these areas often have the biggest impact on the quality of your interactions, which tend to make any discomfort you may feel well worth it. The more you experience the benefits that come from flexing, the less influence style gaps have on you. You begin to see things through a new lens, understanding what people need and responding with more empathy.

As the head of HR, Rachel often has difficult conversations with people, which has given her ample opportunity to flex her Harmonious style. "I used to dread having conversations around performance before I understood communication styles and how to flex to the needs of other styles. Understanding how to approach people allows me to get my message across more effectively. I can establish a much better connection when I shift how I approach the beginning of the conversation and use their style to guide how I deliver information."

The same can be true for you too. The flexing strategies that follow capture the most important areas for style modifications, based on the needs of each style and where there are natural differences. It provides a great starting point for identifying and bridging gaps.

EXPRESSIVE—FLEXING YOUR STYLE

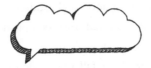

Expressives have a need to personally connect, openly share what they think, and tell you how they feel about everything. They bring an energy and enthusiasm that enlivens every interaction, and, coupled with their confidence and assertiveness, they often assume the lead. These can be wonderful traits but be aware that Expressives frequently create friction with other styles when they become too dominant, move too quickly, and fail to listen.

Flexing to Reserved

Given the contextual nature of the Reserved style, you may find there are times when conversations flow with ease and other times that they feel more challenging. Build on the aspects you have in common: You're both personable and you care about building strong working relationships. You also share an affinity for exploring potential paths by discussing different points of view.

Where you may see a gap between your communication styles is in how you go about building your working relationships. People with a Reserved style prefer to keep things professional and can be more serious in how they approach relationships at work. They also like to have more privacy and prefer to show less emotion, where you enjoy being open with your thoughts and feelings. Look to see if making a few adjustments in some of these areas will help to create smoother and more productive interactions.

Keep discussions professional. As much as possible, restrict your discussions to business topics. Avoid conversations that tread into personal territory and limit your use of humor. Reserved types like connecting with others when it facilitates productivity and relates to tasks. Keep the discussions focused on advancing the work. They care a lot about the quality of their work and want to make sure that everything that needs to be covered in a meeting is adequately addressed. Reserveds take their responsibilities seriously; to build trust, demonstrate that you do too.

Talk less. Listen more. Your talkative style can dominate a conversation and make it difficult for a Reserved to feel heard. Make your point, then open up the floor for others to share. Sit back and listen, resisting your urge to jump back in to build on what others say. During video or conference calls, try using mute to remind yourself to be more intentional about when you chime in.

Slow to a moderate pace. While people with the Reserved style are good at processing information and are comfortable thinking on their feet, they prefer a steady pace. If you slow your tempo just a bit, you'll find a more productive pace that allows you to make more progress than if you push them too hard.

Provide context. Reserved styles like to thoughtfully approach every situation and consider the unique aspects before deciding or choosing a course of action. Provide additional background that will help them understand the most important aspects. When sharing information, be sure to zoom out so they can see the full scope of a situation, then zoom in so they can understand things in detail. This will allow them to see how they can best support others. Remember, Reserved people value their position as a member of the team.

Seek and value their input. Everyone wants to feel like their opinions matter, but having influence is very important to those with a Reserved style. Be sure to acknowledge their position and contribution to the decision process, especially when it helps shape the outcome. Remember, when you flex your style around decision-making, it's about how you approach the process, it's *not* about conforming or caving on your position.

Flexing to Direct

You have a lot in common with people who are Direct! For one thing, you're both confident in your abilities and you communicate with self-assurance. You're able to advance conversations with ease and speed, comfortable expressing a difference of opinion, and reining in conversations that wander too far off topic. Your desire to achieve makes it easier for your styles to get along. Leading also comes naturally to both of you, so it's good to watch for times when you're both attempting to direct a situation.

Where your styles are more at odds is when it comes to how you like to work, approach conversations, and build relationships. Direct people like to work independently and have a strong need to keep discussions brief and focused. In contrast, your love for collaboration, talking things through, and telling stories can frustrate them. They're also very punctual, like to get straight to the point, and stay on task. Your tendency to run late (or just in time) can get things started off on the wrong foot.

When you're flexing toward a Direct style, lean on the qualities you share and identify how to bridge the gaps that create unnecessary tension.

Be punctual and stick to the agenda. I cannot stress this enough: Nothing bothers a Direct more than lateness or running over because of tangents or long stories. Make it a point to start and stop on time. You might even want to set an agenda. Directs love to know what's on deck in advance and to have one in hand to guide the conversation.

Come prepared. Think through your position in advance and anticipate their questions. These aren't people who indulge "winging it." For them, this isn't only frustrating but unprofessional. They're highly conscientious about the quality of their work and expect the same of others.

Limit small talk and stories. You're skilled at putting people at ease, and a little warm-up goes a long way with those who are Direct. That said, they have no need for extensive small talk, so keep it to a minimum. Be warm and approachable, but once you've made a connection, dive right in. Keep communication brief: conversations, Slack, emails, and meetings. The shorter the better.

Keep the conversation focused on work. Direct people are results-driven and task-oriented. They value keeping the conversation focused solely on business. They enjoy discussions that advance the work and lead to better solutions, and they become frustrated when the conversation veers off track.

Share thoughtful perspectives. Precision and accuracy are qualities that define how they think and operate. When sharing your perspective, keep it grounded in facts and logic. They're not often moved by emotional arguments, so be sure to lay a solid foundation before sharing how you *feel* about things.

Listen up. Pay close attention when they're speaking to let them know you respect their knowledge and input. They take their work seriously and want to be heard. In group situations, avoid any side conversations that telegraph that you're not paying attention or don't care about what they have to say.

Ask for their recommendation. Flexing your style around decision-making is about the approach you take *not* about changing or abandoning your opinion. When it comes to making decisions, Directs would rather decide independently. They feel it's faster and they trust their own judgment. Your styles are vastly different in this respect.

When you're leading a decision process, ask them to share their recommendation and rationale, and give them the time they need to think it through and feel prepared. Keep the exchange focused and demonstrate that you're listening.

Watch for power struggles. Given that you're both assertive and confidently share your perspectives, you'll want to watch for situations where you're both trying to lead. Directs are known for arguing their viewpoint until they feel heard. When you see this happening, temporarily dial back your intensity and speak more conditionally. Listen closely to understand what's driving their position and look for ways to come to agreement.

Flexing to Harmonious

You share a number of communication qualities with the Harmonious style that make flexing to this style easier. You're both people-focused and enjoy making personal connections through small talk. You have a common desire for creating smooth, successful teams where people feel supported and encouraged. You both excel at reading people and situations. And you share the ability to keep things lighthearted.

Where you differ and may find communication more challenging is in the areas of assertiveness and speed. While you enjoy sharing your thoughts and opinions, Harmonious people are much quieter. An Expressive will say what comes to mind and deliver it at a quick pace and volume that projects confidence. Harmonious people are more deliberate in what they say, and they speak slower, with less intensity; they want and need time to think things through and feel prepared to share their perspective.

Be respectful and even in your tone. Harmonious people need to feel safe and respected when expressing themselves, and your tone can make all the difference. Make sure you're considerate of their position when you disagree and keep your tone even. Your intensity can be overpowering and if they don't feel safe, they're unlikely to share what they're really thinking. And that isn't going to make the situation any better for anyone.

Slow your pace and pause. The speed of your delivery can make it difficult for the Harmonious style to engage—they prefer to reflect before responding, so working in real time can be a challenge. Try slowing your pace and pausing periodically. This allows them to stick with you and creates an opening for them to jump into the conversation, which is important when you're trying to understand what they're thinking and get to agreement.

Talk less. Create space. And draw them into the conversation. Your ability to lead the conversation can be a real benefit for both of you, provided you make room for them. You may need to invite them to share their thoughts and perspectives, but doing so will create a more balanced discussion—just be careful not to put them on the spot! Try asking questions to pull them into the conversation or talking less to give them a chance to join in. Pay attention to how often you want to speak and rein it in when needed to strike a good balance. Try speaking only once for every three times you want to say something and see if that creates the space needed for a genuine conversation.

Listen with empathy. Listen for the full meaning behind their words to make sure you fully hear and understand them. Ask questions to clarify or try summarizing what you've heard and sharing any assumptions you've made to make sure you're on the same page. Harmonious people are far better listeners than Expressives and they will feel (and appreciate!) when you give them your full attention.

Be patient and watch for interrupting. The slower pace of the Harmonious style can feel challenging to your quick tempo. Watch for showing impatience or judgment through your body language or pace. Take a breath. Stay tuned in. Be patient and allow them to share insights and opinions. Resist the urge to jump in! Let them finish completely before you build on what they've said. If you cut them off too often, they're likely to feel that you don't value what they have to say, which will only make it harder for them to speak up in the future.

Dial back your assertiveness. An Expressive is at the opposite end of the spectrum from a Harmonious person when it comes to how assertively they express themselves. Watch for pushing too hard or coming across with too much force; they're likely to shut down. Keep your tone even and your body language open. Avoid making statements that take a hard stance or leave little room for disagreement or differing opinions.

Give them time to process. If you're planning to have a conversation that leads to a decision, send the materials in advance so they can think things through. Harmonious people need time to process and are very deliberate in what they say and do. Avoid situations where they feel put on the spot.

Share the decision process. An Expressive likes to take a collaborative approach to decision-making, but is willing to make a decision even if everyone isn't on board. This runs counter to how the Harmonious style would proceed. They prefer to have everyone on board before advancing. There are times when it's necessary to decide and move on, even when everyone isn't on the same page. When these situations occur, explain how the decision was reached and why it was important to move forward before reaching full agreement.

Connecting with Another Expressive Style

It can be challenging to communicate with people who share your style because you have too much in common. Our styles shape the role we play during our interactions and if too many people are playing the same role, that can create conflict. Style differences provide the balance and rhythm that's needed for a productive give-and-take in a conversation.

When you're communicating with another Expressive, you may find it easier to temporarily adopt the characteristics of your secondary style, or flex toward another style, to complement each other where you're too similar.

The more self-aware you become of your communication needs and those who share your style, the more readily you'll see where you're likely to run into issues. You'll also become more adept at recognizing the challenges in the moment; in these situations, listen more closely to hear what's needed. Try using some of the flexing techniques below that work well to resolve the most common issues you're likely to face within your own style.

Watch for power struggles. Given that you're both assertive and confidently share your perspectives, you'll want to watch for situations where you're both trying to lead. When you see this happening, temporarily dial back your intensity and let them take the reins.

Watch the time. Your shared love for telling stories and going off on tangents can make it challenging to stay on track and achieve what you set out to accomplish. Try using an agenda with time parameters to keep the conversation focused *and* lively.

Listen up. Expressives are often thinking about what they'll say next, so make it a point to pay attention when they're speaking to let them know you respect their perspective. It's difficult to advance a discussion if you're both talking (a lot!) and neither is really listening.

RESERVED—FLEXING YOUR STYLE

The Reserved style is confident, comfortable speaking up, and enjoys being an influential member of the team. They excel at building professional relationships and advancing the work. Where they run into tension with other styles is when they become too serious, emotionally guarded, or move too slowly. Learning to lighten up, open up, and pick up the pace will help bridge the style gaps that can make it more difficult to build trust with their colleagues.

Flexing to Expressive

Shifting toward an Expressive style can be a challenge for you since you share only a few communication traits. Still, leaning into the areas where you overlap can go a long way to make your interactions easier. You're both very personable and care about building strong working relationships. Exploring potential paths and discussing different points of view is another aspect of communication that you both enjoy.

Your styles are more distinct when it comes to *how* you build your working relationships. People who are Expressive are very open with their thoughts and emotions at work. They're high-energy, animated, and like to make work more fun whereas you prefer to keep things more professional and take a more serious approach. They're also far more assertive and respond best in situations where people are engaged and even push back when they have a different perspective.

They enjoy lively discussions and have little respect for a pushover. Having and voicing your opinion is one of the ways to build trust with an Expressive.

Read through all the approaches to see which temporary adjustments will work best to make your interactions easier and more productive.

Make a personal connection. An Expressive enjoys getting to know the people they work with, so take a few minutes to make a personal connection at the beginning of your conversation. Choose one or two things ahead of time that you're willing to share—maybe you have pets in common, for example, or a sport or hobby that you both enjoy talking about. Open up a bit more and share some of your personal interests in a way that feels comfortable for you. Remember to ask Expressives questions about themselves too—they want you to get to know them.

Share how you feel. Emotions play a large role in how an Expressive communicates. They're quick to let you know how they feel about issues, and they want to know how you feel too. If you're excited about issues, say so! When you're concerned, let that be known too. Expressing your emotions doesn't require a long conversation: you can use your tone, facial expressions, and body language to convey your feelings.

Bring energy and enthusiasm. Expressives love it when others bring energy into the conversation. They're highly enthusiastic and like working with people who share their excitement and enliven work. Dialing up your energy and enthusiasm during your interactions will telegraph that you have confidence in your ideas and passion for your work. Talk with some intensity and use inflection for emphasis. When you meet in person, energize your body language. Lean in and use slightly larger gestures. And it always helps to maintain eye contact and smile.

Pick up your pace. People with the Expressive style like to move fast. They speak quickly, process information quickly, and enjoy conversations that move quickly. They find it easier to communicate with people who move at a fast pace, so keep the speed of the conversation high.

Keep things light. Expressives care about delivering high-quality work just like you do, but they like to have fun while they do it. They prefer an informal, lighthearted approach—that proverbial spoonful of sugar that makes work feel less like work. Engage in a lighter manner when it's appropriate. Even smiling more and opening up your body language will go a long way. By taking a more relaxed approach, you'll create a better connection.

Have a point of view. An Expressive is more assertive and quicker to let you know what they're thinking, and they want to know where you stand. Voicing your perspective is one way to build trust with an Expressive. If you disagree, say so. If there's a problem, raise the issue early on. They like to get things out in the open and find solutions that get things back on track. They want to see the team running smoothly.

Carve out enough time for the conversation. An Expressive is the most talkative and outgoing of all the styles. They often like to think out loud and explore the potential of ideas. They like to jump from topic to topic and can sometimes pull a conversation off track. Allow them some room to move the conversation around; if the parameters become too confining, they're likely to feel restrained and become irritated.

Give them some airtime. Communicating energizes Expressives, and they're often unaware of the fact that they tend to dominate the conversation. Let them take the lead, and be tolerant if the discussion takes a detour (or two). Bonus points if you can demonstrate active listening. While Expressives like to steer the conversation, they also want to know that you're listening and engaged.

Ask questions. Expressives are known for asking questions. It's one way that they engage with people and deepen their connections during a discussion. Asking a question in return is one way to show that you're interested in their perspective.

Come prepared to decide. An Expressive likes to take a collaborative approach to decision-making. They sincerely want to hear from everyone, and it will go a long way if you come prepared to discuss your perspective.

Flexing to Direct

People who are Reserved tend to get along well with those who are Direct because you're both quite serious about your work and like to keep the conversation on task. Neither of you enjoys a lot of small talk or wants to wade into your personal lives or those of your coworkers. You also appreciate that you're both thorough and come fully prepared for every conversation. These traits, along with your mutual desire to reach your goals, bring you together.

When flexing to a Direct style, you want to focus on aligning with their pace and assertive communication behaviors. They like to move more quickly than you do and may become frustrated if you move too slowly or conditionally. By temporarily applying a few of these behavioral shifts, you'll create more effective interactions and build more trust.

Be on time and be brief. Make it a point to start and stop on time. Being late and running over irritates a Direct person more than any other style. Dive into the subject of conversation as soon as possible. They like communication to be clear and concise: conversations, emails, and meetings; the shorter the better. When you've finished the discussion, gracefully wrap it up and move on.

Keep it high-level. Avoid getting into details with a Direct person. They have less interest in all the contextual layers that you like to delve into. Keep your conversation focused on the big picture; if they need more information they won't hesitate to ask.

Pick up the pace. They process information quickly and move at a quick clip. Speak faster than you normally would; this will help them stay engaged and feel like the conversation has been an efficient and effective use of their time.

Ask for their recommendation and provide options. When it comes to making decisions, ask them to share their recommendation and rationale. This approach addresses their preference to independently direct the outcome and your need to have a lot of context before deciding. To be clear, flexing your style around decision-making is about the approach you take and does *not* require you to abandon your opinion.

Say what you think. The Direct style is candid and straightforward. They prefer a tell-it-like-it-is approach. Proactively share your perspective and let them know where you stand. They find it annoying to have to ask people to join in the conversation and, in fact, they're more likely to ignore and devalue those who don't vocally share their opinion.

Address conflict. Neither of you likes to address conflict, but allowing things to fester or waiting for problems to clear up on their own is only going to make matters worse. If there's something bothering you, or a problem that needs to be solved, raise the issue.

Flexing to Harmonious

You sync up with the Harmonious style in some key areas. You both like to play a supporting role on a team and build strong working relationships. Neither of you are overly assertive, and you both prefer to avoid unnecessary conflict. You're also similar in the fact that you're able to keep your cool and manage your emotions well at work.

Where your needs tend to differ is when it comes to connecting on a deeper level and showing more support and warmth. The Harmonious style is very supportive of others and expects everyone to provide the same level of care that they show. While you're more guarded in displaying your emotions, they want to have conversations that help them feel like they know you and understanding how you feel is vital to them.

The tips below will help you to bridge the main gaps between your styles and help someone who's Harmonious feel more comfortable.

Be respectful and supportive. Harmonious people need to feel safe and secure when expressing themselves—your tone can make all the difference. Make sure you're respectful of their position when you disagree and keep your tone even. If you come across as overly confident or dismissive, it can make them become cautious, and it's unlikely that they'll share what they're really thinking.

Pause now and then. Your steady pace is more aligned with the needs of the Harmonious style, who likes time to process information. Still, they're unlikely to interrupt you and pausing will create the opening they need to ask questions. This will help them feel more comfortable stepping into the conversation and help you understand what they're thinking.

Listen with empathy. Harmonious people are the best listeners, and they know when you're tuned in. Set aside your viewpoint and try to see things from their perspective. Stay open and curious. They will appreciate (and feel) when you give them your full attention.

Take the lead to kick things off. They're more cautious and deferential in conversations, and naturally on the quiet side. Since neither of you care to assume the lead, initiate the conversation to get things rolling. Share your perspective and ask to hear theirs. They prefer to spend more time listening than talking and may need to be drawn into the conversation, especially when you're in a group setting.

Add some warmth. Harmonious people are quite caring and enjoy developing close working relationships. Use a warm tone and open body language to convey a friendly and warm demeanor.

Give them time to process. If you're planning to review information to reach a decision, send the materials in advance so they can think things through. Harmonious people need time to process and are very deliberate in what they say and do. Avoid situations where they feel put on the spot.

Engage them in the decision-making process. They think a lot about how decisions affect people and like to have everyone on board before advancing. When possible, spend time discussing the options and how it will impact others, so they can see you've taken people's needs into account. Of course, sometimes it's necessary to make a real-time decision to keep business moving. When these situations occur, explain how the decision was reached and why it was important to move forward before reaching full agreement.

Connecting with Another
Reserved Style

It can be challenging to communicate with people who share your style because you simply have too much in common. Style differences create the balance needed in a conversation and provide roles that make it easier to build productive working relationships. When you're communicating with another Reserved person, you may find it easier to adopt the characteristics of your secondary style, or flex toward another style, to complement each other in places where you're too similar.

The more self-aware you become of your communication needs and those who share your style, the more readily you'll see where you're likely to get stuck around issues or run into conflict. You'll also become more adept at recognizing the challenges in the moment; in these situations, listen more closely to hear what's needed. Try using some of the flexing techniques that work well with Expressive and Direct styles, both of which are more assertive and complement the most common issues you're likely to face within your own style. Below are flexing techniques that work well to resolve the most common issues you're likely to face with another Reserved.

> **Provide context.** You both like to have a fair amount of background before determining a course of action, so one of you is going to need to step up and provide the background for both of you. Come prepared with the information you'll both need to advance the discussion.

Take the lead around decisions. Reserved people like to weigh in on the decision-making process, but they don't want to be responsible for making the final call. When you're collaborating with another Reserved and need to reach a decision, one of you will need to be more assertive and make the decision.

Watch for playing it too safe. Reserved types aren't comfortable taking risks. Pay close attention to being too cautious when you're generating new ideas, setting goals, or making decisions.

DIRECT—FLEXING YOUR STYLE

People who are Direct are quite candid, independent, and achievement-focused. They like to move at a quick pace; the more they accomplish, the better they feel. They take their responsibilities quite seriously and inspire higher levels of accountability in others, but if they're not careful, they can come across as impersonal and dominant. Their desire to dive right into work and keep the conversation on task can create tension with styles that need to make a personal connection—to feel seen and heard—in order to build trusted working relationships.

Flexing to Expressive

You share many communication behaviors with people who have an Expressive style. You are both quite confident in your abilities and express yourself with self-assurance. You advance conversations with ease and speed. You both enjoy leading and are more assertive than others, meaning you're comfortable expressing a difference in opinion and reining in conversations that wander too far off topic. Your need for achievement also brings you together.

Where your styles may be at odds is when it comes to how you approach conversations and build relationships. Expressives love to work in teams and collaborate, but you prefer working independently. They're high-energy, like to think out loud, and have personal conversations and tell stories. You like to get straight to the point and keep things brief and professional. Below are tips that cover the biggest gaps between your styles. When you flex toward an Expressive, temporarily applying a few of these techniques will make your conversations more effective and productive.

Use small talk to make a personal connection. Use the first few minutes before a meeting to make a connection with an Expressive. They need a warm-up lap around the track before they feel ready to dive into the work. They genuinely want to know you. Open up and share personal interests or a story in a way that feels comfortable for you. And be sure to ask them about themselves; they want you to get to know them too. It doesn't have to be long, but trying to jump right in will start things off on the wrong foot.

Bring some energy and enthusiasm. They love it when others bring some energy into the conversation and enliven work. They're highly enthusiastic and like working with people who share their excitement. Dial up your energy and enthusiasm when you're connecting. Talk with some intensity and use inflection for emphasis. When you meet in person, energize your body language. Lean in. Use slightly bigger gestures.

Keep things light. Expressives care about delivering high-quality work just like you do, but they also like to make work more fun. They prefer an informal approach—that proverbial spoonful of sugar makes work feel less like work. Engage in a lighter manner when it's appropriate. Even smiling more and opening up your body language will go a long way.

Share how you feel. An Expressive is quick to let you know what they're thinking and feeling, and they want to know where you stand. Emotions, in particular, play a large role in how they communicate. Open up a bit and proactively share your perspective. If you're excited about something, say so. When you're concerned, let it be known. Expressing your emotions doesn't require a long, deep conversation; you can even use your tone, facial expressions, and body language to convey most of your feelings.

Carve out enough time for the conversation. An Expressive is the most talkative and outgoing of all the styles. They often like to think out loud and explore the potential of ideas as a group. Communicating energizes them, and they're often unaware of the fact that they tend to dominate the conversation. Let them take the lead, and be tolerant if the discussion takes a detour (or two). If the conversation strays too far, gracefully pull it back around to the subject at hand. They'll appreciate the gesture when it's handled well.

Cut them some slack if they run late or run over. Expressives are known for getting caught up in a conversation and losing track of time. This causes them to be tardy for meetings, as well as running over the allotted time frame. They mean well, so assume a positive intent. They don't enjoy running behind and will appreciate it if you can smoothly help keep meetings on track.

Show you're listening. Everyone wants to feel heard, but an Expressive watches to see if you're listening. While they often like to control the conversation, they also want to know that you're listening and engaged. Stay tuned in and show that you're interested in their perspective, even when it's wrapped in a story. It's one way to deepen your connection during a discussion and build trust.

Ask for their input. When it comes to making decisions, ask them to share their input and then discuss it. Allow the conversation to wander a bit; Expressives often connect the dots by jumping from one point to the next. This approach addresses their preference to take a collaborative approach to decisions. Just remember, flexing your style around decision-making is about the approach you take, and doesn't require you to abandon your opinion.

Watch for power struggles. Given that you're both assertive and confidently share your perspectives, you'll want to watch for situations where you're both trying to lead or dominate. Expressives want to feel heard and respected, which can create a power struggle if you both dig your heels in. When you see this happening, temporarily dial back your intensity and speak more conditionally. Listen closely to understand what's driving their position and look for ways you can come to agreement.

Flexing to Reserved

Your Direct style shares a lot of similarities with people who are Reserved. You both take your responsibilities seriously and like to keep conversations on task. Neither of you enjoys a lot of small talk, and you believe that the personal lives of your coworkers are their business and not a subject of discussion at work. You build your professional relationships through the work you accomplish together. Your mutual desire to perform at your best and achieve strong results builds trust.

When flexing to a Reserved style, you want to focus on strengthening your relationship by providing more context, slowing your pace, and listening to their input. Reserveds like to have influence and be seen as a valuable member of the team, so be sure to give them a chance to weigh in. By temporarily applying just a few of these techniques to close your style gaps, you'll create more productive interactions and build a stronger relationship.

Share the big picture and details. Reserveds like to see the full picture and care about the strategies as well as the tactics. When sharing information, zoom out so they can see the full scope and then zoom in so they can understand things in detail. Giving them context, or sharing information ahead of time, will make them feel they have the information they need to do the job, make a decision, or see how they can best support the team.

Seek and value their input. Everyone wants to feel like their opinions matter, but having influence is especially important to those with a Reserved style. Be sure to acknowledge their position and contribution to the decision process, especially when it helps shape the outcome. Even when you disagree, let them know that you value their perspective. Flexing your style around decision-making doesn't mean you need to modify your opinion or adopt theirs; it's about letting them know you have heard them and taken their view into account.

Slow to a steady pace. You naturally communicate and move at a faster pace than someone who's Reserved. While they're good at processing information and comfortable thinking on their feet, they prefer a slightly slower pace. If you ease up on your tempo just a bit, you'll hit a productive groove that allows you to make more progress than you would by pushing them too hard.

Flexing to Harmonious

You share only a few communication behaviors with the Harmonious style, and this is admittedly one of the more challenging flexes. Your common ground lies in your practicality and deliberate approach to how you engage with people. You're both more guarded in expressing your emotions, but for very different reasons: You feel that your personal feelings aren't relevant to the work at hand, whereas Harmonious people value knowing the feelings of others but they're reluctant to share their own.

There are several style gaps between you, but the biggest are around the way you build relationships and your pacing and decision-making. Harmonious people are more cautious and deferential; they prefer to listen and like to get everyone board before deciding, whereas you like to lead and assume responsibility and are happy to make decisions independently, even if everyone isn't in agreement. They need time process information, and you like to keep a quick pace.

They care about supporting others, while you're known for being independent and self-sufficient. Given that your styles are quite different, temporarily flexing your style in a few ways that meet more of their needs will significantly improve the quality of your working relationship.

Be respectful and supportive. Harmonious people need to feel safe and secure when expressing themselves—your tone can make all the difference! Make sure you're respectful of their position when you disagree and keep your tone even. Your directness can make them feel uncomfortable—irritated or insecure—and they're likely to disengage or withhold what they're really thinking.

Slow your pace and pause. The Harmonious style prefers a slower pace, which can feel challenging to your quick tempo, but moving too quickly or making them feel put on the spot will only backfire. Pause periodically to give them an opportunity to digest what you've said. They won't interrupt you, so pausing creates the openings they need to ask questions. Watch for showing impatience or judgment through tone or body language. Take a breath. Stay tuned in, and be patient so they can share their insights and opinions.

Listen with empathy. Listen for the meaning behind their words to make sure you fully hear and understand them. Ask questions to clarify or try restating what you're hearing to make sure you're on the same page. You often see situations quite differently, and factoring in their perspective can round out and strengthen yours. Harmonious people value listening to others and they will appreciate (and feel) when you give them your full attention.

Dial back your authority. Harmonious styles defer to authority and become quieter, more cautious, and deferential when you come on too strong. If your goal is to engage them (which it should be!), avoid pushing them too hard or forcing a decision. Watch for making statements that take a hard stance or leave little room for disagreement.

Give them time to process. Try to avoid situations where they feel put on the spot. Harmonious people need time to process and are very deliberate in what they say and do. If you're planning to review information and reach a decision, send them the materials in advance so they can think things through.

Draw them into the conversation. You may need to invite them to share their thoughts and perspective if they feel you have greater command of the situation. Harmonious people prefer to spend more time listening than talking and often need to be drawn into the conversation, especially in a group setting.

Add some warmth. The Harmonious style is very people-oriented. They genuinely care about their coworkers and enjoy developing close working relationships. By approaching your interactions with more warmth and friendliness, you'll help them engage more fully, which will create more productive connections.

Engage them in the decision-making process. Harmonious styles think a lot about how decisions impact people and they like to have everyone on board before advancing. When possible, spend time discussing the options and how it will affect others, so they can see you've taken the human needs into account. Of course, sometimes it's necessary to make a real-time decision to keep business moving. When these situations occur, explain how the decision was reached, how you considered the people side of things, and why it was important to move forward before reaching full agreement.

Connecting with Another
Direct Style

It can be challenging to communicate with people who share your style because you have too much in common. Our styles create the roles we play during our interactions and if too many people are playing the same role, it inevitably creates conflict. Style differences provide the balance and rhythm that's needed for a productive give-and-take in a conversation.

When you're communicating with another Direct person, you may find it easier to temporarily adopt the characteristics of your secondary style, or flex toward another style, to complement each other where you're too similar.

The more self-aware you become of your communication needs and those who share your style, the more readily you'll see where you're likely to run into issues. You'll also become more adept at recognizing the challenges in the moment; in these situations, listen more closely to hear what's needed. Try using some of the flexing techniques that work well to complement the most common issues you're likely to face within your own style. Below are flexing techniques that work well to resolve the most common issues you're likely to face with another person who has a Direct style.

> **Thoroughly evaluate your decisions.** Given that you're both quick to make decisions and are focused on creating results, be sure you're thinking through the long-term implications and consider the human side of things. Your business mindset may lead you to overlook the impact that your decisions have on people and how

others will be affected by the changes you're implementing.

Intentionally collaborate. Working independently is your preferred approach, which can make collaborating with someone else who's Direct more challenging. One of you will need to take the lead to plan times to touch base, exchange ideas, and make sure your thinking is aligned.

Invest in building the relationship. Your intense work ethic and ability to stay on task may drive faster results initially, but if neither of you invests in building the relationship beyond work transactions, your productivity will suffer over time. Create some time to foster a connection and build rapport so you can maintain a good working relationship.

Watch for power struggles. Given that you're both assertive, confident, and deliberate, you'll want to watch for situations where you're both trying to lead or dominate. When you see this happening, simply allow them to take the reins. Listen closely to see if there's anything other than style needs driving their approach, and continue to look for ways you can keep advancing the work without letting power dynamics get in the way.

HARMONIOUS—FLEXING YOUR STYLE

People who are Harmonious are naturally agreeable, cooperative, and patient. They value keeping the peace and building strong working relationships, and care about supporting people. They're quite deliberate in what they say and do, and they need more time to process information and think through their perspective before speaking up. They're good listeners and don't feel the need to dominate the conversation. They're also conflict-averse and would rather comply than create a disagreement that could damage a relationship. When engaging with more assertive styles, Harmonious people can come across as too quiet, too cautious, and too agreeable, which can create tension with other styles and erode trust.

Flexing to Expressive

You share a number of communication qualities with the Expressive style that puts you in natural alignment. You are both highly people-focused and like to build personal and professional relationships that often extend outside of work. You like to encourage people, understanding that this helps to create high-functioning teams. You share the ability to hear what goes unsaid and can read a room quickly. You also both appreciate adding levity to situations when they start to feel heavy or tense.

Your styles differ when it comes to your level of assertiveness, your openness to sharing your emotions and opinions, and how fast you speak and process information. Expressives are quick to share their thoughts, feelings, and perspectives about everything, and this isn't your preference. You're more deliberate in your approach, choosing to thoughtfully consider what you'll say and how it will land before you speak. Expressives, on the other hand, speak with confidence and an intensity that can feel overpowering to you at times.

Bring some energy and enthusiasm. Expressives love it when others bring more energy into the conversation and work. They're highly enthusiastic and like working with people who share their excitement. Increase your energy and enthusiasm when you're connecting. Talk with some intensity, use inflection for emphasis, and energize your body language if you're meeting in person. Gestures as subtle as leaning in, smiling, or nodding emphatically can speak volumes.

Pick up your pace. People with the Expressive style like to move fast. They speak quickly, process information quickly, and enjoy conversations that move quickly. They find it easier to communicate with people who move at a quick clip, so pick up the pace of the conversation to match theirs whenever you can.

Share how you feel. Emotions play a large role in how an Expressive communicates. They're quick to let you know where they stand and how they feel about issues, and they want to know where you're at, too. Open up a bit more to let them know how you feel. If you're excited about something, say so. When you're concerned, let it be known. If things are moving too quickly and you feel pushed, gently let them know what you're experiencing. You can also use your tone, facial expressions, and body language to convey your feelings. And if they don't pick up on your signals, be sure to say something, especially when you feel uncomfortable. Honoring how you feel, and expressing it with grace, helps build respect and trust with an Expressive.

Come prepared to decide. An Expressive likes to collaborate and discuss options before making a decision; they will readily share their opinions and they want to hear yours. Come prepared to share your perspective and be one of the first to speak up to elevate your presence. Even when you agree be sure to tell them why. Otherwise, they may misread your agreement as passiveness, which can annoy an Expressive.

If you disagree, say so. An Expressive prefers to step into disagreements and discuss any differences in order to work through problems. They're more assertive and like to get things out in the open. An Expressive is quick to let you know what they're thinking and feeling, and they expect the same from you. If there's a problem, raise the issue early and be clear. Proactively share your point of view. They want to see the team running smoothly and find it tiresome to have to ask people to join in the conversation or share their position on a matter.

Flexing to Reserved

You share quite a few communication behaviors with the Reserved style that make your interactions easier; you're both team players, like to build strong working relationships, and are supportive of the people you work with. You're both deliberate about how you engage with people and like to have enough background information before choosing your position or taking action. Additionally, you share the ability to keep your cool when tensions rise, providing more stability in difficult situations.

When flexing to a Reserved style, limit small talk and stay in a professional space while looking for opportunities to show your engagement. They take work seriously and want to work with people who care about performing at their best. They're also adept at processing information and thinking on their feet, so come prepared. One area where your styles actually align but can be problematic is around leadership—neither of you loves to be at the helm—so you may need to step into this role to get things moving. The tips below will help you to bridge the main gaps between your styles and strengthen your relationships with people who have the Reserved style.

Keep discussions professional. Stay true to your friendly nature but avoid asking personal questions. People who are Reserved like to keep things on a professional level. As they get to know and trust you, they may open up more. If you let your relationship unfold on their terms, it will be stronger.

Come prepared to engage. People who are Reserved like to engage in discussions that deepen their understanding and keep the work moving. They're adept at processing information, thinking through multiple perspectives, and forming their opinions in real time. Come prepared to confidently share your perspective; they'll want to know where you stand on issues as they're discussed.

Take the lead. Since neither of you cares to assume the lead, initiate the conversation to kick things off. Share your perspective and provide added context; they like to understand the factors that shape your opinion. Make sure you leave with a clear understanding of any next steps so you know you're in agreement and can continue to make progress.

Seek and value their input. Everyone wants to feel like their opinions matter, and having influence is very important to those with a Reserved style. Seek their input when making decisions and let them know it's appreciated.

Flexing to Direct

The Direct style is the furthest away from your style preferences, but you do share a few qualities that you can build on. You both prefer to limit how much you share when it comes to expressing your emotions. You're both quite deliberate in what you say and do, preferring to be seen as thoughtful and practical rather than spontaneous. Building on this common ground between you can help bridge some of the larger gaps between your styles.

You have several style differences that show up around assertiveness, connections, pacing, and relationship building. The Direct style will readily disagree if they have a different perspective, where you'd prefer to agree to protect the relationship and avoid conflict. They don't like small talk; you do. They like to work and make decisions independently, whereas you like to work and decide collaboratively. They process information quickly; you need time to think things through. Given that your styles are quite different, there's a lot to be gained by temporarily flexing your style in ways that meet the needs of someone who's Direct, and in doing so, you can significantly improve trust and raise the quality of your working relationship.

Pick up your pace. Directs speak quickly, process information quickly, and enjoy conversations that move quickly. They find it easier to communicate with people who move at a faster clip, so pick up the pace of the conversation to match theirs where you can.

Limit small talk. Keep the warm-up period of the conversation brief. Directs have no need for small talk, so once you've made a connection, dive in.

Be brief and keep things moving. Directs process information quickly and care about managing their time. Whether it's an in-person conversation, email, or meeting, the shorter the better. Eliminate stories that may be interesting but are, ultimately, unnecessary. Once you've finished the discussion, gracefully wrap it up and move on.

Come prepared. Be ready to hit the ground running in a meeting. Set an agenda, think through your position, and anticipate what questions may arise. The Direct style will be frustrated if you're unprepared, too quiet, or too agreeable. They're highly conscientious about the quality of their work and expect everyone to demonstrate equal engagement.

Keep the conversation focused on work. Direct people are results-driven and task-oriented. They value keeping the conversation focused on business. They enjoy discussions that advance the work and lead to better solutions, and they become frustrated when the conversation veers off track.

Express yourself with confidence. Demonstrate self-assurance and belief in your perspective. Directs often have strong opinions and if you're too agreeable it will irritate them. Speak with more certainty and project confidence through your body language: maintain a strong posture and look them in the eye.

Speak up. Engage actively in the conversation and let Directs know where you stand. Initiate the discussion from time to time too, so they don't feel like they have to keep seeking your input or drawing you into the conversation.

If you disagree, say so. Directs like to get things out in the open and prefer you have a differing opinion than none at all. This may be uncomfortable for you but preparing your approach in advance will make it easier.

Connecting with Another
Harmonious Style

It can be challenging to communicate with people who share your style because you have too much in common. Our style differences create the balance needed in a conversation and provide distinct roles that make it easier to build productive working relationships. When both people are vying for the same role it can create problems.

When you're communicating with another Harmonious person, you may find it easier to temporarily adopt the characteristics of your secondary style, or flex toward another style, to complement each other where you're too similar.

The more self-aware you become of your communication needs and those who share your style, the more readily you'll see where you're likely to run into issues. You'll also become more adept at recognizing the challenges in the moment; in these situations, listen more closely to hear what's needed. Try using some of the flexing techniques below to address the most common issues you're likely to face within your own style.

Take a stance. Your agreeable nature often keeps both of you from being the first to share an idea, take a firm position, or share a dissenting point of view, which limits your progress and prevents richer discussions and better solutions. Be prepared to take a stance and be more decisive, so you can advance the discussion in a meaningful way.

Lead the conversation. If you're both waiting for the other to lead it will be difficult to make progress, feel a sense of accomplishment, or achieve your goals. Be willing to provide direction and guide the conversation.

Watch for playing it too safe. People who are Harmonious are fairly risk-averse. Watch for being overly cautious when you're generating new ideas, setting goals, or making decisions.

Keep things moving. Since you both prefer a slower pace, when you're working on projects together you may find that the momentum stalls or you miss deadlines. Make it a point to bring more energy and drive to your interactions so you keep things moving. Agree on who will own what aspects of the project and what needs to be delivered by when. As the saying goes, agreements prevent disagreements.

Conclusion

𝒞 ommunication is the birthplace of human connection, collaboration, creativity, and change. It's a powerful force in our work lives—and it's hard to overestimate the positive impact that communication can have on your well-being and sense of purpose. Even small changes can alleviate stress, which raises your baseline level of well-being and creates a virtuous cycle that allows you to be open, collaborate more effectively, and see new possibilities. When we're able to do our best work, we're more likely to enjoy what we do and to have a positive impact on the people and world around us.

This might sound a little grand, but it's true. Remember, the ability to find more purpose in your work begins by becoming more purposeful in the way you interact with *people*. It's about living aligned with your values and expressing yourself at that level. And because we have to communicate in our job every day, we're all constantly presented with opportunities to put the practices we've learned into action and become more consciously aware of how we engage with people.

It doesn't take long to experience the benefits of raising your communication skills. People will feel a difference right away when you actively listen and intentionally respond. And so will you! The more familiar you are with your style, the more you play to your strengths; the better you understand your triggers, the better prepared you can be when they come up; the more aware you are of whether you're staying above the line, the more readily you can clear the air and stay accountable to yourself. Together, these pillars of elevated communication—raising self-awareness, fostering well-being, and forging trusted relationships—can help you to decrease burnout, improve productivity, and create a positive impact. They can help you to thrive in all your working relationships.

Now, I know it's tempting to close this book and put it on a shelf, but building communication skills isn't a one-and-done deal! The reality is that real change simply doesn't happen by reading a book. It's my sincere hope that as you continue to explore your communication style that you'll *apply* the insights you've gained to continually evolve and elevate your communication skills. If you find you slip back into old patterns—like staying up too late, interrupting people, or avoiding a difficult conversation—just come back and check in to see what you need. We all slip and slide a bit when we're growing; progress isn't a linear path. What matters most is that you catch yourself and get back on the path again.

The ability to understand yourself and build new skills takes time and dedication. The old adage "practice makes perfect" is cliché for a reason: You have to consistently, intentionally practice until your new skills are second nature. This means creating simple daily rituals to activate the ideas until they become ingrained in your brain's neural chemistry. Start small and build. Moment by moment, day by day, we strengthen our awareness, we learn, and we evolve; it's the microevolution of Self that connects you to more and more of your potential.

There's no endgame when it comes to awareness. There's always another layer to be revealed, new insights to discover, new experiences to reflect on. Elevating your communication skills is a process. As your conscious awareness expands, you'll find that it's much easier to see your style, recognize when you're slipping into stress, and shift your behavior to stay above the line. My hope is that you continue to enjoy learning about yourself and strengthen your well-being so that you can be at your best more often and enjoy what you do.

As you continue on this journey to elevated communication, never lose sight of the fact that your emotions and behaviors are infectious and your influence exponential. When you play to your strengths and express yourself from the healthy side of your style, you have the ability to bring out the best in others.

And every time you have a positive interaction with your colleagues, you're unconsciously shaping the behavior within your team, organization, and community. The change you want to experience begins with you.

I'll leave you with this thought: We live in a world that's filled with uncertainty, but there's one constant you can always count on, and that's change. The world is going to continue to change and I believe for the better. Each of us has the ability to do our part to positively influence the direction of that change. And if we're going to find meaning through our work, we have to develop strong communication skills. We need to elevate the way we engage and keep moving to the next level.

This requires that we understand ourselves and others and actively build healthy relationships that keep us connected. And it's much easier to do this work when we've got a community that supports us. So, tell others about the things you're figuring out about yourself and share your insights with your friends. Invite them to discover their communication style—the assessment is free—and to join you on this journey. Life is infinitely easier and much more fun when you surround yourself with people who want to grow.

Thank you for joining me on this journey, consciously bringing your voice into the world, and making it a better place.

Acknowledgments

It has been an incredibly humbling experience to take an idea for a book and bring it into form. I've learned so much throughout this process, and what has become abundantly clear is that collaboration is the true genius behind any creative endeavor. I'm eternally grateful for all the guidance, love, and encouragement I've received along this journey. Your belief in me kept me going when the full realization of what I'd taken on hit me in wave after wave (after wave).

Before I ever experienced the transformative power of communication in the world of business, I experienced its true magic within my family. My love and appreciation for my husband, Mike Hancuch, and my children, Will and Kate, have no limits. The openness, love, and genuine connection we've cultivated through conscious communication has been life-changing. You've taught me what's truly possible through intentional communication. Having you in my life means everything, and you make me ridiculously happy every day. Thank you!

This book would not have been possible without the enormous talents of Paul Riedesel, whose brilliant mind for research and ability to extract meaning from reams of data helped me to discover the four communication styles. Thank you for developing a sophisticated algorithm that now makes it easy for people to find their style. I'm so grateful our paths crossed at Fallon so long ago and that we could work together once again.

Thank you to the entire team at Tiller Press and Simon & Schuster who made this book a reality. I'm eternally grateful for the clear vision and inspiring leadership of Theresa Dimasi and her talented group—Patrick Sullivan, Laura

Acknowledgments

Flavin, Lauren Ollerhead, Molly Pieper, Kate Davids, Kayla Bartee, Sam Ford, Laura Levatino, Annie Craig, Benjamin Holmes, and Dominick Montalto—who provided their support along this journey. And a huge thank-you to Hannah Robinson, whose editing guidance and support made all the difference in the world. You helped me to find my voice and appreciate the power the power of simple anecdotes. I loved working with you!

My heartfelt gratitude also extends to the family and friends who've believed in me, shared their stories, provided insights, and offered their talents in support of creating this book and a better world for us all. I'm so thankful for Gingy O'Brien, Rosemary O'Brien, Dondeena Bradley, Maureen Higgins, Joan Steffend, Liz Koumantzelis, Tara Pereyl, Chris Naylor, Rachel Soffer, Beth Perro-Jarvis, Amy Arias, Lisa Hannum, Rebecca Martin, Amye Zemke, Amy Clark, and Kevin Wong. I'm so blessed to have you all in my life!

To all the teachers and guides who taught me to listen within, be myself, and bring all of who I am into the world, thank you for providing the inspiration, courage, and nudge I needed at just the right moment. This includes an endless list of authors for whom I hold the deepest admiration and appreciation; the truths and wisdom shared through their work have helped to shape who I am and who I'm becoming.

Lastly, to all the readers who've made it this far and are working to elevate their communication skills, thank you for bringing more empathy and understanding for yourself and others into your daily conversations and the world of business (and beyond). *Who you are* is already making a profound difference in this world!

Notes

CHAPTER 1:
Communication Is at
the Heart of Our Success

1. GMAC Research Team, "Employers Still Seek Communication Skills in New Hires," MBA.com, July 30, 2020, https://www.mba.com/articles-and-announcements /articles/your-career-path/employers-seek-communications-skills.

2. Mike McDonald, "How Having a Best Friend at Work Transforms the Workplace," Gallup, October 16, 2018, https://www.gallup.com/cliftonstrengths /en/249605/having-best-friend-work-transforms-workplace.aspx.

3. Elaine Houston, BSc, "The Importance of Positive Relationships in the Workplace," *Positive Psychology*, October 13, 2020, https://positivepsychology.com /positive-relationships-workplace/.

4. Perry E. Geue, "Positive Practices in the Workplace: Impact on Team Climate, Work Engagement, and Task Performance," *Journal of Applied Behavioral Science* 54, no. 3 (September 2018): 272–301, DOI: 10.1177/0021886318773459.

5. Emily D. Heaphy and Jane E. Dutton, "Positive Social Interactions and the Human Body at Work: Linking Organizations and Physiology," *Academy of Management Review* 33, no. 1 (2008): 137–62.

CHAPTER 2:
Meet Your Brain

1. Bruce H. Lipton, PhD, *The Biology of Belief: Unleashing the Power of Consciousness, Matter & Miracles* (New York: Hay House, 2008).

2. Joe Dispenza, DC, *Evolve Your Brain: The Science of Changing Your Mind* (Deerfield Beach, FL: Health Communications, Inc., 2007).

3. Bruce H. Lipton, PhD, "Dr. Bruce Lipton Explains How to Reprogram Your Subconscious Mind," YouTube, July 9, 2019, https://www.youtube.com/watch?v=OqLT_CNTNYA.

4. Sharon Linde, "Reticular Activating System: Definition & Function," Study.com, August 23, 2016, https://study.com/academy/lesson/reticular-activating-system-definition-function.html.

5. Shahram Heshmat, PhD, "What Is Confirmation Bias?" *Psychology Today*, April 23, 2015, https://www.psychologytoday.com/us/blog/science-choice/201504/what-is-confirmation-bias.

6. Albert H. Hastorf and Hadley Cantril, "They Saw a Game: A Case Study," *Journal of Abnormal and Social Psychology* 49, no. 1 (1954): 129–34, https://doi.org/10.1037/h0057880.

7. Jim Loehr, *The Power of Story: Rewrite Your Destiny in Business and in Life* (New York: Free Press, 2007).

8. Dan Baker, PhD, and Cameron Stauth, *What Happy People Know: How the New Science of Happiness Can Change Your Life for the Better* (New York: Rodale, 2003).

9. Dispenza, *Evolve Your Brain.*

10. Joe Dispenza, PhD, "TED Talks with Dr. Joe Dispenza," YouTube, February 8, 2018, https://www.youtube.com/watch?v=W81CHn4l4AM.

11. Dr. Joe Dispenza, *Breaking the Habit of Being Yourself: How to Lose Your Mind and Create a New One* (New York: Hay House, 2012).

Notes

CHAPTER 3:
We're All Connected

1. Gregg Braden, "A Great Mystery Is Solved! What's Shaking Up the Scientists?" HealYourLife.com, December 10, 2009, https://www.healyourlife.com/a-great -mystery-is-solved.

2. Christopher L. Kukk, PhD, *The Compassionate Achiever: How Helping Others Fuels Success* (New York: HarperCollins, 2017); David Loye, *Darwin's Unfolding Revolution and the Liberation of the 21st Century* (self-published, 2004), https://www .thedarwinproject.com/revolution/book/dur.pdf.

3. Rollin McCraty, PhD, *Science of the Heart: Exploring the Role of the Heart in Human Performance*, vol. 2 (Boulder Creek, CA: HeartMath Institute, 2015).

4. David R. Hawkins, MD, PhD, *Truth vs. Falsehood: How to Tell the Difference* (New York: Hay House, 2005).

5. Sigal Barsade, PhD, "Faster Than a Speeding Text: 'Emotional Contagion' at Work," *Psychology Today*, October 15, 2014, https://www.psychologytoday.com /us/blog/the-science-work/201410/faster-speeding-text-emotional-contagion-work.

6. Sourya Acharya and Samarth Shukla, "Mirror Neurons: Enigma of the Metaphysical Modular Brain," *Journal of Natural Science, Biology and Medicine* 3, no. 2 (July–December 2012): 118–24, https://www.ncbi.nlm.nih.gov/pmc/articles /PMC3510904/.

7. Dispenza, *Breaking the Habit of Being Yourself.*

CHAPTER 4:
Staying Tuned In

1. Stephanie Vozza, "Six Habits of the Best Conversationalists," *Fast Company*, April 6, 2016, https://www.fastcompany.com/3058579/six-habits-of-the-best -conversationalists.

2. Dream McClinton, "Global Attention Span Is Narrowing and Trends Don't Last as Long, Study Reveals," *Guardian*, April 17, 2019, https://www.theguardian.com/society/2019/apr/16/got-a-minute-global-attention-span-is-narrowing-study-reveals.

3. Bob Sullivan and Hugh Thompson, *The Plateau Effect: Getting from Stuck to Success* (New York: Dutton, 2013).

4. Nancy K. Napier, PhD, "The Myth of Multitasking," *Psychology Today*, May 12, 2014, https://www.psychologytoday.com/us/blog/creativity-without-borders/201405/the-myth-multitasking.

5. Roman Krznaric, "Six Habits of Highly Empathic People," *Greater Good Magazine*, November 27, 2012, https://greatergood.berkeley.edu/article/item/six_habits_of_highly_empathic_people1.

6. Erik C. Nook, Desmond C. Ong, Sylvia A. Morelli, Jason P. Mitchell, and Jamil Zaki, "Prosocial Conformity: Prosocial Norms Generalize across Behavior and Empathy," *Personality and Social Psychology Bulletin* 42, no. 8 (May 2016): 1045–62, https://journals.sagepub.com/doi/10.1177/0146167216649932.

CHAPTER 5:
Understanding the Communication Styles

1. C. G. Jung, *Psychological Types* (Princeton, NJ: Princeton University Press, 1974).

CHAPTER 7:
Mastering Your Communication Style

1. Tasha Eurich, *Insight: The Surprising Truth about How Others See Us, How We See Ourselves, and Why the Answers Matter More Than We Think* (New York: Currency, 2017).

2. Nancy Olson, "Three Ways That Handwriting with a Pen Positively Affects Your Brain," *Forbes*, May 15, 2016, https://www.forbes.com/sites/nancyolson /2016/05/15/three-ways-that-writing-with-a-pen-positively-affects-your-brain /?sh=7206694f5705.

3. Eurich, *Insight*.

4. Jennifer Porter, "Why You Should Make Time for Self-Reflection (Even If You Hate Doing It)," *Harvard Business Review*, March 21, 2017, https://hbr .org/2017/03/why-you-should-make-time-for-self-reflection-even-if-you-hate -doing-it.

CHAPTER 8:
Renew Your Energy

1. World Health Organization, "Burn-Out an 'Occupational Phenomenon': International Classification of Diseases," WHO.int, May 28, 2019, https://www .who.int/news/item/28-05-2019-burn-out-an-occupational-phenomenon -international-classification-of-diseases.

2. Jen Fisher, "Workplace Burnout Survey," Deloitte, 2015, https://www2.deloitte .com/us/en/pages/about-deloitte/articles/burnout-survey.html.

3 37. Ibid.

4. "Want to Be More Productive in 2018? Take More Breaks," *Innovation at Work* (blog), Sloan School of Management, MIT, December 3, 2017, https://executive .mit.edu/blog/want-to-be-more-productive-in-2018-take-more-breaks.

5. Mayo Clinic Staff, "Job Burnout: How to Spot it and Take Action," MayoClinic .org, November 20, 2020, https://www.mayoclinic.org/healthy-lifestyle/adult -health/in-depth/burnout/art-20046642.

6. Centers for Disease Control and Prevention, "1 in 3 Adults Don't Get Enough Sleep," CDC.gov, February 18, 2016, https://www.cdc.gov/media/releases/2016 /p0215-enough-sleep.html.

7. Benjamin C. Holding, Tina Sundelin, Mats Lekander, and John Axelsson, "Sleep Deprivation and Its Effects on Communication during Individual and Collaborative Tasks," *Scientific Reports* 9, no. 3131 (February 28, 2019), https://www.nature.com/articles/s41598-019-39271-6.

8. Veronica Guadagni, Ford Burles, Michele Ferrara, and Giuseppe Iaria, "The Effects of Sleep Deprivation on Emotional Empathy," *Journal of Sleep Research* 23, no. 6 (December 2014): 657–63, https://onlinelibrary.wiley.com/doi/full/10.1111/jsr.12192.

9. Matt Walker, "How Sleep Affects Your Emotions," TED.com, August 2020, https://www.ted.com/talks/matt_walker_how_sleep_affects_your_emotions?language=en#t-58692.

10. Brandon Peters, MD, "First Step to Better Sleep: Wake Up at the Same Time Every Day," VeryWell Health, May13, 2020, https://www.verywellhealth.com/30-days-to-better-sleep-3973920.

11. Sara E. Alger, Allison J. Brager, and Vincent F. Capaldi, "Challenging the Stigma of Workplace Napping," *Sleep* 42, no. 8 (August 2019), https://doi.org/10.1093/sleep/zsz097.

12. David R. Hawkins, MD, PhD, *The Map of Consciousness Explained: A Proven Energy Scale to Actualize Your Ultimate Potential* (New York: Hay House, 2020).

13. Shawn Achor, *The Happiness Advantage: The Seven Principles of Positive Psychology That Fuel Success and Performance at Work* (New York: Crown Business, 2010).

14. Pierre Philippot, Gaëtane Chapelle, and Sylvie Blairy, "Respiratory Feedback in the Generation of Emotion," *Cognition and Emotion* 16, no. 5 (August 2002): 605–27, http://www.ecsa.ucl.ac.be/personnel/philippot/RespiFBO10613.pdf.

15. Rick Hanson, PhD, *Buddha's Brain: The Practical Neuroscience of Happiness, Love & Wisdom* (Oakland, CA: New Harbinger Publications, 2009).

16. Jack Canfield, *The Success Principles: How to Get from Where You Are to Where You Want to Be* (New York: HarperCollins, 2005), 299.

17. Jack Canfield, "5 Tips to Stop Negative Self-Talk Once & for All," *Maximizing Your Potential* (blog), https://www.jackcanfield.com/blog/negative-self-talk/.

CHAPTER 9:
Build Healthy Relationships

1. Houston, "The Importance of Positive Relationships in the Workplace."

2. Calvin D. Banyan, *The Secret Language of Feelings: A Rational Approach to Emotional Mastery* (Tustin, CA: Banyan Publishing, Inc., 2003).

3. Tom Rath and Jim Harter, *Wellbeing: The Five Essential Elements* (New York: Gallup Press, 2010), 34–35.

4. Carolyn Taylor, *Walking the Talk: Building a Culture for Success* (London: Random House, 2005).

5. Clay Blackham, "Costly Conversations: Why the Way Employees Communicate Will Make or Break Your Bottom Line," VitalSmarts.com, December 6, 2016, https://www.vitalsmarts.com/press/2016/12/costly-conversations-why-the-way-employees-communicate-will-make-or-break-your-bottom-line/.

CHAPTER 10:
Elevate Your Approach

1. Jory Mackay, "Weekly Reads: 3 Ways to Improve Communication in the Workplace," *RescueTime* (blog), June 14, 2018, https://blog.rescuetime.com/communication-in-the-workplace/.

About the Author

MARYANNE O'BRIEN has spent decades guiding people and cultures to foster open communication, cultivate empathy, and deepen trust. She has a depth of experience building iconic brands and purpose-driven organizations, and helping businesses to consciously transform. She's worked with big brands like Nordstrom, Coca-Cola, and Apple, as well as small, independent businesses. Her background in advertising, consulting, and corporate coaching taught her to value authentic leadership and healthy cultures, and inspired her to found Conscious Company. Maryanne is dedicated to supporting shifts in conscious leadership, communication, and well-being. She also leads classes in intuition development and energetic healing techniques—mentoring people on a path to higher consciousness. She lives with her husband on a hobby farm just outside Minneapolis, where she leads retreats. Visit her online at Conscious-Company.com.